The Dark Decade
1829–1839

Other book by the author

Yesterday at Kalaupapa

The Life and Times of John Young

Shipmans of East Hawai'i

Hawaiian Stamps: An Illustrated History

The Dark Decade
1829–1839

Anti-Catholic Persecutions in Early Hawai'i

Emmett Cahill

Mutual Publishing

ISBN 1-56647-635-6

Library of Congress Catalog Card
Number: 2004104656

First Printing, October 2004
1 2 3 4 5 6 7 8 9

Design by Jane Hopkins

Mutual Publishing
1215 Center Street, Suite 210
Honolulu, Hawaii 96816
Ph: (808) 732-1709
Fax: (808) 734-4094
email: mutual@mutualpublishing.com
www.mutualpublishing.com

Printed in Korea

Table of Contents

Preface

The persecution of Catholics in the Hawai'i of 1829–1839 was unique if only because nowhere in North America, the nearest landmass, was such intolerance by a governing power inflicted upon a religious sect. There may have been isolated cases but none of them government-sanctioned such as that which occurred in the Kingdom of Hawai'i.

Nor would it have happened in that island nation had not Queen Ka'ahumanu, a zealous supporter of recently-arrived Calvinist missionaries, been persuaded to suppress Catholicism, even to the point of prohibiting the recital of Catholic prayers in a Hawaiian hut. Guided by the hand of the Protestant pioneer, the Reverend Hiram Bingham, her power extended not only to native Hawaiians but also to include the banishment of two French priests. Some years passed before King Louis Philippe of France learned of this action and the insult it perpetrated on his country. He then took harsh steps to bring religious freedom to Hawai'i. While discord did not die overnight, Catholicism was allowed to grow and eventually flourish, but not before the United States Congress was involved and a French frigate trained its guns on Honolulu. Even Great Britain's consul was a leading protagonist.

This author's primary source of information is the *History of the Catholic Mission in the Hawaiian Islands* by Father Reginald Yzendoorn. This Belgian-born priest was a member of the Paris-based Congregation of the Sacred Hearts of Jesus and Mary and at the time of his writing was the chancellor and secretary for what would later become the Catholic Diocese of Honolulu. His work was published at the request of Bishop Stephen Alencastre by the *Honolulu Star-Bulletin* in 1927. Yzendoorn had begun his research as far back as 1908. In the preface to his book, he recounts stories from native Hawaiians who had shown an interest in Catholicism. Yzendoorn first considered writing a novel on the subject but was asked by then-bishop Libert Hubert Boeynaems to put his efforts toward the compilation of the work and progress of the Sacred Hearts fathers in Hawai'i.

Some years earlier, in Paris, the Reverend Marcellin Bousquet, the superior-general of the Sacred Hearts Congregation, had expressed a desire to record the labors of the Catholic fathers in Hawai'i. "It seems that nothing is known of the apostolic labors and the history of the people of Oceania," he wrote. "A missionary who would devote his hours of leisure to the composition of such historical study would thereby perform a task both useful and agreeable to many people."

With this encouragement, Father Yzendoorn reviewed the documents he had on hand and, he wrote in early 1908, "thought I might attempt the task." Five years later he felt the satisfaction of having accomplished the task and that his "years of patient and extensive research would see the light of day." But for reasons unknown, Bishop Libert was not inclined to have the work published. It was only after Libert's death that his successor, Stephen Alencastre, quickly ordered Yzendoorn to publish his manuscript. The task was accomplished in 1927, but not until the contents were updated and a new chapter added. The history "embraced the entire century which had elapsed since the departure of the first Catholic missionaries from France [1826] for the Hawaiian Islands."

In the preface to his monumental work, Yzendoorn wrote that his work was "neither apologetic nor controversial. I have not reproached nor condemned the Protestant missionaries for opposing with all their might what in their opinion is the error of errors."

This author, while relying heavily on Yzendoorn's work, also had access to other sources, especially the *Sandwich Island Mirror* of January 15, 1840. In a special supplement to the newspaper, a non-Catholic author wrote a 34,000-word article entitled, "An Account of the Persecution of the Catholics at the Sandwich Islands."

Although Yzendoorn extracted much from that supplement, he apparently researched his subject extensively. Historian Ralph Kuykendall observed, "For the history of the missionary enterprise, the standard authority is the well-documented work of Fr. Reginald Yzendoorn, *History of the Catholic Mission in the Hawaiian Islands*" (Kuykendall, 139n). Kuykendall also might have added that Yzendoorn accomplished his work with several thousand words less than the early account in the *Sandwich Island Mirror.*

✠ ✠ ✠

Note: Yzendoorn references appear so frequently as citations from his History *that this author has omitted his name in many in-text references, leaving only the page number. Thus (122) is an Yzendoorn citation.*

Chronology

1831   Bachelot and Short summoned to appear before council of chiefs.

1831   Formal order for priests to depart within three months.

1831   Mission press issues condemnation of Catholicism.

1831   Boki and companions lost at sea. His wife, Liliha, as acting governor, deposed by Kaʻahumanu.

1831   Father Bachelot protests formally to Kaʻahumanu of the persecution of native Catholics.

1831   Council of chiefs meet and agree to expel priests.

1831   American Consul Jones and British Consul Charlton send strong letters of support for priests, to no avail.

1831   Formal expulsion. Priests forced aboard vessel *Waverley.*

1832   Priests left on barren California bay of San Pedro. Farmer feeds them, takes them on overnight journey by carriage to San Gabriel Mission.

1832   Father Short moves to Mission San Bautista where he later helps establish a school. Father Bachelot remains in San Gabriel.

1832   Death of Kaʻahumanu. Succeeded by Princess Kīnaʻu since King Kamehameha III is too young to occupy throne.

1837   Under false impression that it was now safe to come back to Hawaiʻi, both priests return on *Le Clemetine.* Governor Kekūanaōa refuses to let the priests land.

1837   Government prohibits sale of alcohol. Closes grogshops to great displeasure of visiting seamen. Vessel *Europa* arrives with a priest, Louis Maigret aboard. Regent Kīnaʻu refuses permission to remain. Arrangements made for vessel *Nôtre Dame de Paix* to carry Bachelot and Maigret to Micronesia.

1837   Father Bachelot, already ill, dies at sea. Father Maigret sees to his burial on Micronesian islet of Napali.

1838	King Kamehameha III signs official document, printed on the Lahaina Protestant press, titled "Rejecting the Catholic Religion." It ran to several pages.
1839	Regent Kīna'u dies at the age of 32. However, her severe persecution of Hawaiian Catholics worsens under new queen regent, Kekāuluouhi. Kamehameha III still considered too young to rule.
1839	Death of de Paula Marin. Catholic funeral services prohibited.
1839	King Louis de Phillipe of France orders French frigate *L'Artiseme* to leave Sidney for Honolulu to avenge treatment of his subjects in Hawai'i.
1839	Chiefs issue "Declaration of Rights." No mention of religion.
1839	Captain Laplace of *L'Artiseme* arrives in Honolulu, issues firm manifesto guaranteeing religious freedom for all residents of Hawai'i under penalty of having Honolulu bombarded. Government consents. Treaty signed July 12.
1839	August, King Kamehameha III, finally able to rule, gives his people full rights to worship as they please.
1841	U.S. representative Baird has audience with King Louis Phillipe on behalf of Protestant Mission. King supports new turn of events in Hawai'i.
1859	Anglican Church established in Hawai'i, but only after many months of warding off objections from Boston-based American Board of Protestant Missions.
1900	Catholic churches and schools well-established in Hawai'i.

CHAPTER ONE

Early Catholic Presence

Legend, tradition and documented evidence lend credence to the theory that Catholicism touched the Hawaiian Islands well before the arrival of the French priests in 1827. This concept dates to the life of a religious leader who lived in Hawai'i centuries before the advent of Europeans.

Though the mists of time have obscured much of the origins and life of the kahuna (priest) Pā'ao, tradition gives him an important place in Hawai'i's early history—"early" meaning as far back as the eleventh century. Polynesian historian Herb Kane writes in his *Voyagers*, "About the time William the Conqueror crossed the English Channel, Pā'ao logged no less than eleven thousand miles on his voyage of conquest" (Kane, 59). He also indicates that Pā'ao came from Ra'iatea in the islands of Tahiti, to which he made at least one return trip.

Historian Abraham Fornander, who contends that Pā'ao came from Samoa, fixes his arrival in Hawai'i in the twelfth century (Fornander, 30, in Yzendoorn, 10).

Another well-known historian of the middle nineteenth century, Samuel Kamakau, suggests that the great Pā'ao had his origins in New Zealand (*Ka Nupepa Kuokoa*, 29 December 1866, in Yzendoorn, 9–10).

More interesting than his place of birth are Pā'ao's ethnic origins. He has more than once been described as a white man. Father Reginald Yzendoorn writes that "the unanimous affirmation of all witnesses to Hawaiian tradition, by calling him a 'haole', and a white man, expressly precludes the hypothesis of Sawaiori origin." He adds that "no Europeans crossed the Pacific at an earlier date than the Spaniards, from which it may be concluded that Paao...belonged to that nationality" (11).

It is through the Reverend William Ellis, early English missionary and Hawai'i historian, that credence is given to Pā'ao having been a Catholic, and possibly a Catholic priest instead of a Polynesian kahuna, as some have identified him.

About 1823, Ellis heard from native Hawaiians that "a kahuna arrived at Hawaii from a foreign country; that he was a white man, and brought with him two idols or gods, one large, and the other small; that they were adopted by the people, and placed among the Hawaiian gods; that the above-mentioned temple of Mookini [on the north end of Hawai'i Island] was erected for them, where they were worshipped according to the direction of Paao, who became a powerful man in the nation." The Mo'okini temple which Ellis mentions was, the Hawaiians told him, "celebrated in the historical accounts, as built by Paao, a foreign priest, who resided in Pauehu, and officiated in this temple" (Ellis, 283).

Ellis further writes, "The most unaccountable circumstance connected with the priest Paao, is his having arrived alone, though he might be the only survivor of his party. If such a person ever did arrive, we should think he was a Roman Catholic priest, and that the reported gods were an image [statue] and a crucifix" (ibid., 320).

There is no indication of the Catholic faith being practiced in Hawai'i at that time, and if it was, it did not survive. As for Pā'ao, it can be said that he remains a historical question mark.

Stronger evidence of a Catholic presence comes from Ellis' belief, and that of other historians, that the Spanish reached Hawai'i three hundred years earlier than the French priests who came in the 1800s. One of the leading theories is that they accidentally came across the Hawaiian archipelago while sailing their galleons between Acapulco and Manila. Spanish ships carried silver from the mines of Mexico to Manila, and from Manila brought back to Spain such riches as spices, porcelain, silk and other prizes of the Orient.

Ellis was told of a painted ship without masts or a sail, making an appearance. One leader on board wore a hat with a feather in it. Another wore at his side a large *pahi*, or a broad sword. Their clothes were white or yellow (ibid., 319–20).

Historian William D. Alexander wrote, "There is little doubt that these islands were discovered by the Spanish navigator, Juan Gaetano, in the year 1585." Alexander cites, and Yzendoorn quotes, documents in the archives of the Spanish Colonial Office in Madrid that refer to Gaetano (or Gaytan) naming the islands. One, presumably Hawai'i Island because of the smooth top of Mauna Loa, was called La Mesa, or Table. Others were identified as Los Monges (The Monks or Friars Islands). Maps and charts of these islands with their Spanish names are in the Madrid archives (Alexander, 99, in Yzendoorn, 12).

A thorough overview of the Spanish trade in the Pacific is found in Kane's *Voyagers* (Kane, 77ff.). He tells not only of hundreds of galleons that crossed the Pacific, but also of the trade routes they followed to avoid British and Dutch privateers. It is significant that these routes had no reason to bring them near the Hawaiian Islands which were as yet unknown to Europeans. Those that did encounter the islands never established a colony or any form of government. Nonetheless, there is evidence that Spanish men left their mark, for in the years after 1600 there is mention of light-skinned men among the population, along with their fair-complexioned offspring. Ellis surmises that early

Spanish arrivals may have been shipwrecked "or culprits committed by their countrymen to the mercy of the waves" (Ellis, 320). On Kaua'i, Captain Cook's men discovered pieces of iron, one being the tip of a broad-sword, all evidence of earlier European visitors. Bolstering the Spaniard theory is a stone bust of a man found on the island of O'ahu, said to date from before Cook's arrival. "It represents a European gentleman, whose circular ruff, pointed beard and standing mantelet collar are of the fashion which prevailed between 1580 and 1630" (Yzendoorn, 13). The original statue ended up in Bremen, Germany. A cast of the subject is in the Bishop Museum in Honolulu.

While the details are murky regarding galleons that may have stopped and any settlers who stayed, these newcomers no doubt brought some aspect of their faith with them, perhaps even in the form of a chaplain aboard one of the sailing vessels. Yet while charts and documents testify to the presence of these ships, no tangible vestige of the Catholic religion was left behind except the name Monges Island.

Still, Yzendoorn provides a more positive analysis. Studying both the time of Pā'ao and the presence of Spaniards, he concludes, "It seems then that there can be little doubt that the strangers of the Hawaiian legends are Spaniards, and that consequently Paao and Pili belonged to that nationality... Now since Paao introduced a new religion, it can hardly have been any other than the Catholic religion" (14). The case, however, is weak, and if it was Catholicism, none of it rubbed off and remained.

A more positive presence of the Catholic religion is a matter of record. But like the story of Pā'ao and the Spanish experience, the faith did not take hold. In 1819, the French vessel *L'Uranie* visited the islands under the command of Captain Louis Claude Desaules de Freycinet. Just four months after the death of Hawai'i's King Kamehameha I, the ship anchored off Kawaihae. There it attracted the attention of the high chief Kalanimoku.

He boarded *L'Uranie* and asked his adviser John Young about the functions of the man he saw garbed in vestments. Young explained that he was the ship's chaplain, the abbé de Quélen, and described his role as a Catholic priest. Kalanimoku said he wished to become a Christian like Young, and asked if he could be baptized. It was arranged that the services would take place the following day, and with due ceremony.

The young King Kamehameha II, Liholiho, also was present "donned in a blue with gold trimmed uniform of the hussars, furnished with a thick colonel's epaulets..."; he was attended by four others from his court. Freycinet's journal tells of having sent to Liholiho "...my pinnace to this purpose, and soon we saw him appear, accompanied with the five queens...and the princess Ka'ahumanu, a long procession of pirogues with the ladies and gentlemen of his court followed in his wake...I saluted the monarch on his arrival with eleven guns. The quarter deck was decorated with flags...The favorite queen and Ka'ahumanu were seated on chairs in front of the altar which had been erected on deck. Finally the abbé de Quélen, with the usual ceremonies, baptized Kraimoku, [Kalanimoku] who during the whole proceedings showed a deep emotion" (de Freycinet, 538, in Yzendoorn, 19). It was August 14, 1819. Kalanimoku chose Louis as his baptismal name after Captain Freycinet, who acted as his godfather. After an exchange of presents the royal party took leave.

It is easy to understand why Kalanimoku's faith did not endure, for there was no Catholic clergy to offer instruction or the sacraments. Although Yzendoorn says that the new convert may have obtained a knowledge of the Christian religion, it is understandable that Kalanimoku, upon the arrival of the Protestant missionaries six months later "showed them favor" (Yzendoorn, 19). Six years later, in 1826, they admitted him to church membership, but did not re-baptize him, considering his French baptism valid. Kalanimoku died in March 1827, four months before the arrival of the priests.

When *L'Uranie* arrived in Honolulu, Governor Boki of O'ahu, a younger brother of Kalanimoku, having learned of his brother's baptism, insisted the same privilege be granted him. Accordingly Father de Quélen baptized him on August 27, 1819, and gave him the name of Paul. "In him the members of the Catholic Mission, who were to arrive eight years later, were to find a willing colleague...," who kept their adversaries, particularly Ka'ahumanu, at bay till he himself was removed from the scene of Hawaiian history by an ill-fated adventure (20).

It has been said that a Spaniard, Don Francisco de Paula Marin, lent a somewhat Catholic presence to Honolulu, where he made his home for the last forty-four years of his life. But the evidence is slim, unless one counts the great number of individuals(more than three hundred), who, it is said by Marin himself, he had baptized. The converts were mostly children whose parents had called upon him to provide medical assistance, and he baptized them secretly to ensure salvation for their souls should they die.

He was perhaps a practicing Catholic prior to his arrival in Hawai'i about 1793. There he would find no clergy to say Mass or otherwise help him keep his faith. The fact that he had two wives and fathered about twenty children would not have endeared him to the fathers of his faith when they arrived in 1827. Some of his descendants live in Hawai'i today (Day *Biographical*, 94).

Born in 1774 in Andalusia, Spain, Marin proved himself over many years in Hawai'i to be a man of many interests and skills: agriculturist, botanist, merchant, accountant, interpreter, physician and advisor to visiting ship captains. "A man of great versatility Marin served his friend the king" in a number of ways. He was, as one knowledgeable in medicine, called to attend Kamehameha on his death bed (ibid.).

Honolulu's very modern Vineyard Boulevard is so-called because of Marin's sizeable grape orchards. Near Honolulu's waterfront, a street near his early dwelling perpetuates his name. Yzendoorn says of him, "His mind was a strange mixture of pagan beliefs...but he never forgot his boyhood faith. As a visiting doctor in the community he was said to have saved more than three hundred souls from hell by secretly baptizing patients." He was cautiously friendly with the Protestant missionaries who arrived in 1820 but became suspicious of their strictness; nor was he trusted by the Catholic clergy when he was reluctant to aid them" upon their arrival (ibid.).

Regardless of whether there is any truth to his assertion to the artist Arago that he had baptized more than three hundred souls, it is a fact that the first thirteen baptisms registered in the early Catholic Mission records were performed at Marin's residence by a Mexican merchant four months before the arrival of the French priests.

There is evidence that as a "lapsed" Catholic, Marin rejoined his church after the arrival of the priests. Marin's contribution to a Catholic presence in the islands perhaps was peripheral, but may have been commendable considering all those baptisms.

Though it can hardly be considered a "Catholic presence," there was in Honolulu before the French arrival a small number of Catholics consisting of both foreigners and natives. However, without a priest and a place of worship, it could hardly be called even the nucleus of a Catholic community for it would have been neither canonical nor liturgical.

Chapter Two

The Coming of the Calvinists

Aside from the arrival of the westerners with Captain Cook in 1778, there is perhaps no more significant day in the annals of Hawai'i, for better or worse, than April 1, 1820.

On that day, after a voyage of 164 days from Boston via Cape Horn, the brig *Thaddeus* made landfall on Hawai'i Island in the far-off Sandwich Islands. Captained by Andrew Blanchard, with First Officer James Hunnewell, the ship carried the Protestant missionary group of two ordained ministers and their wives plus five lay members of the American Board of Commissioners for Foreign Missions (ABCFM) and their wives. The Chamberlain family also included five children. In addition, there were three young Hawaiians who had been helpers at the Cornwall Foreign Mission School in Connecticut and were returning home. Most of the group were young and on the long voyage they had to contend with homesickness as well as seasickness.

The missionary band was prepared to do battle with Satan. Its immediate and long-range goal was to save the heathen Hawaiians from themselves and from sin. This Pioneer Company, as it was known, was the first of twelve companies that the ABCFM would send to the Sandwich Islands over the next twenty-eight years. Each of the missionary men and women had been trained at the Cornwall Foreign Mission School. This first missionary band came well prepared. Twenty-nine-year-old Elisha Loomis was a printer who would soon be at work with his type and a Ramage press. Another non-ordained missionary was Thomas Holman, a physician who was a medical school graduate and who had also trained at the Cornwall Foreign Mission School. Daniel Chamberlain was "to teach the natives agriculture and the mechanical arts" (HMCS, 7). The appointed (some said self-anointed) head of this First Company was the Reverend Hiram Bingham, who, with his wife, remained in Hawai'i in a leadership capacity for twenty-one years.

The Protestant missionaries could not have arrived at a more propitious time. Everything was in their favor. Kamehameha the Great had been dead for almost a year. With the passing of this longtime ruler also passed the many sacred taboos that the king had respected and expected his followers to do the same. But these many strict prohibitions and customs were discarded shortly after the ceremonials that followed the king's death.

The new youthful king, Liholiho, now Kamehameha II, lacked the leadership qualities of his father and the late king's favorite wife, Ka'ahumanu. She was a strong-willed person who became a co-ruler with the successor king. What the missionaries found was a vacuum, a ship of state minus its religious rudder. Surely, they reasoned, this had been divined and designed by the Almighty.

However, they were not welcomed with open arms. Liholiho took his time in granting them permission to land. Some of the chiefs in council favored allowing them to settle. Others had their doubts. But permission eventually was granted, though on a probationary basis as suggested by John Young, the confidant and advisor to his late friend Kamehameha I. But dig in they did, mostly in Honolulu, with missionary outposts established elsewhere in the archipelago. With this foothold, they lost little time in setting up schools that launched a long educational legacy in the islands, one well-laced with Puritan practices and ideals.

During the early years that followed, Bingham became a powerful influence on the Hawaiian way of life, albeit a somewhat unpopular one with the white population who were affected by his strict Christian code, particularly in Honolulu. Bingham, with the many missionaries who followed, had much to say not only on matters moral, but eventually about the educational and political affairs of the small nation. In doing so he opened himself to criticism not only from some Hawaiians who found him overly zealous, but from the foreigners as well.

Early on, Ka'ahumanu was persuaded to accept the teachings of Christ as presented by the Reverend Bingham. She was baptized on December 4, 1825. To their credit, the missionaries soon gained many members, not only adults but also young students attending in thatched structures that served as schools. The Congregational religion soon became the state religion.

This attachment to the state was contrary to the formal instructions set forth by the ABCFM whose board showed concern for the welfare of those who were to be proselytized. Its instructions to the missionaries were clear on the method of promoting their spiritual goals. The instructions read in part:

> You are not to be limited to a low, narrow scale; but you are to open your hearts wide and set your marks high.
>
> You are to aim at nothing short of covering these islands with fruitful fields, and pleasant dwellings and schools and churches, and of raising up of the whole people to an elevated state of Christian civilization.

You are to obtain an adequate language of the people; to make them acquainted with letters; to give them the Bible with skill to read it.

To introduce and get into extended operation and influence among them, the arts and institutions and usages of civilized life and society; and you are to abstain from all interference with local and political interests of the people and to inculcate the duties of justice, moderation, forbearance, truth and universal kindness.

Do all in your power to make men of every class good, wise and happy

(HMCS, 17)

Many years later, the author and traveler Richard Henry Dana testified in a letter to the *New York Tribune* that the missionaries had, for the most part, accomplished much of what they set out to do. Dana stated that,

in the space of forty years they have taught this whole people to read and write, to cipher and to sew. They have given them an alphabet, grammar, and dictionary; preserved their language from extinction, given it a literature and translated into it the Bible and works of devotion, science and entertainment etc. etc. They have established schools, reared up native teachers, and so pressed their work that now the proportion of inhabitants who can read and write is greater than in New England ... and the more elevated of them taking part in conducting the affairs of the constitutional monarchy under which they live, holding seats on the judicial bench and the legislative chambers, and filling posts in the local magistrates.

(Dana, June 5, 1860)

What is not documented is that the ABCFM Instructions to abstain from political interference did not foresee intrusion by "those Papists," the Catholics. It was to become a matter of holy competition, and Bingham held his ground by engaging the official support of Queen Ka'ahumanu, who had become an ardent convert.

Nearly a quarter of a century later, when Bingham retired to the United States, he wrote *A Residence of Twenty-One Years in the Sandwich Islands*. It remains a historical source of information of the culture and times of that period, the early part of the nineteenth century.

CHAPTER THREE

The Queen Regent of Hawai'i

Kaahumanu was born with her world in her hands...She was entwined in blood with the high chiefs of Maui and Hawaii. [It was] prophesied that someday she would be a ruler "and all your relatives will bow in your presence"

(Silverman, 1)

This powerful chiefess was born about 1768 in Hāna on the island of Maui, the daughter of regional rulers Ke'eaumoku and Nāmāhana. All who saw her agreed that she was beautiful. One of those was Kamehameha the Great, then a powerful chief on Hawai'i Island, who chose her as one of his wives.

She was young at the time, probably in her mid-teens. She soon became his favorite wife and remained so until the king's death in 1819. The great navigator George Vancouver was among those who commented upon her beauty when she accompanied her husband to His Britannic Majesty's ship *Discovery*. (Some say the comments about her beauty were not reflected in the likeness of her as sketched by the French artist, Louis Choris). Ka'ahumanu was proud, liked to set the style, loved beautiful things and took pains to show her rank.

After Kamehameha's death in 1819, Ka'ahumanu, with the help of the young King Liholiho and Keōpū'olani (Kamehameha's most sacred wife because her lineage was higher than his), lost little time in destroying the many *kapu* which governed the daily lives of the Hawaiians. About this time, "...Ka'ahumanu created for herself the new post of kuhina nui, roughly, executive director" (Daws, 55).

When Keōpū'olani gave birth to Liholiho, Ka'ahumanu was made *kahu*, or custodian, of the child. For the rest of his short life, even as king, Ka'ahumanu retained the role as co-ruler or *kuhina nui*. (Following the early death of Liholiho she became sole ruler.)

Although Prince Liholiho inherited the throne, historians agree that he lacked the leadership skills of Kamehameha the Great. He also lacked his father's political and administrative acumen, as well as his athletic abilities and military prowess.

As King Kamehameha II, Liholiho sailed with his favorite wife, Kamāmalu, for England. They departed Hawai'i on November 27, 1823. With them were members of their court and the young Frenchman, Jean Baptiste Rives, an entrepreneur and landholder in Hawai'i. He was also a confidant and secretary to Kamehameha II and his services as interpreter in England would be necessary. Rives also had up his sleeve a plan to visit France, to persuade the Catholic church officials to send French priests to the Sandwich Islands.

But Liholiho's plans for British collaboration with the Hawaiian Kingdom fell apart, for shortly after their arrival in London in July 1824, both Hawaiian sovereigns were felled by measles. It was a disease for which they had no immunity. They died within a week of one another. The royal party returned to Hawai'i on the ship *Blonde* which bore the bodies of Liholiho and his queen, Kamāmalu. Conspicuous by his absence was Jean Rives who departed for Paris to press his plan to bring Catholic priests to the Sandwich Islands, and the possibility of material gain for himself.

After the demise of Kamehameha II, next in line for the symbolic Hawaiian throne was Kauikeaouli, the second son of Kamehameha I and Keōpū'olani. The boy was only eleven years old, too young to reign. Thus Ka'ahumanu became, with the approval of the chiefs, the ruler, with the high chief Kalanimoku as prime minister. In no time she became known to many as the Queen Regent. She had learned well from her husband and teacher to organize, to administer and to rule. And rule she did, with a rod of iron, until her death in 1832.

It was only a matter of days after the 1820 arrival of the New England missionaries that their leader, the Reverend Hiram Bingham, first made contact with Liholiho and, soon after, Ka'ahumanu. At that time Ka'ahumanu was one of the most powerful persons in the kingdom. There were those who were higher by birth, and there were those who were higher by title, but probably not one held greater influence.

Samuel Kamakau wrote that Ka'ahumanu became one of the first converts to the new Kawaiaha'o Protestant church. On December 4, 1825, she had been baptized and took the Christian name of "Elisabeta." Prior to that she had shown signs of embracing Christianity by making a tour of O'ahu, visiting her people, entering even the most humble of huts and exhorting the natives to obey the word of the new God.

After her baptism she became a fully fledged member of the Kawaiaha'o church. The Reverend Bingham, who had given her instruction, was pleased that his convert soon became a zealous Christian. She had the support of many of the chiefs when, in a speech to the people in December 1825, she told them, "You must obey the laws of Jehovah, keep the Sabbath day holy and be obedient to the word of God, for by doing so we shall have salvation" (Kamakau, 322).

Again quoting Silverman:

Ka'ahumanu reintegrated religion at the center of law and

chiefly order...Building on her rank and the political power
of her family, she had gained her stature and authority in
secular matters. She had done away with the traditional
religion and consolidated her secular rule before she moved
to adopt the new religion.

(Silverman, 130)

There is little doubt that Ka'ahumanu considered the
missionary brand of Christianity as central to authority and it
was her role to comply and have her subjects do likewise. Thus
her expectation that they would all attend Sabbath services.
Kuykendall states that "By 1840 Hawaii was officially a Christian
nation," but of one religious denomination only (Kuykendall, 115).
Though this was eight years after the queen's demise, she had
earlier set the tone and pace, with Bingham at her ear. And
Princess Kīna'u, her successor, was every bit the rigid religious
enforcer that Ka'ahumanu had been.

Bingham has been criticized for his interference in matters
of state, thus disregarding the Instruction from the ABCFM
board not to become involved with local and political interests.
Any difference between the affairs of church and the affairs of
state were to become very blurred to the point where later
historians labeled Congregational and Presbyterian teachings
as the state religion. In this, Ka'ahumanu as regent had
considerable support of many chiefs who, while not converts,
were influenced by missionary teaching. Possibly to show her
feeling toward deceased pagan chiefs, she traveled early in her
reign to Hōnaunau on Hawai'i Island to demolish Hale o Keawe
(temple) and had the chiefs' bones burned "and the house
broken down" (Kamakau, 285).

With Kauikeaouli, the heir to the throne, too young to
administer affairs of state, Ka'ahumanu was the recognized ruler
until her death eight years later. Those eight years (1824–1832) would
see much change. It was not long after her baptism that Ka'ahumanu

would promulgate what would today be labeled Blue Laws. Her prohibitions against the manufacture, sale or consumption of liquor angered the foreign population, particularly the sailors, who protested to Bingham. His response was to go see Ka'ahumanu, as "She made the law," But undoubtedly she acted at Bingham's urging. Aside from liquor prohibitions, the queen decreed:

> You shall not commit murder; he who puts another to death shall also die.
>
> You shall not commit adultery; he who commits this crime, man or woman, shall be banished to Kaho'olawe.
>
> You shall not practice prostitution; anyone guilty of this shall be imprisoned and beaten across his back with a rope, and if he still fails to keep the law shall be banished to Kaho'olawe.
>
> (Kamakau, 288).

In December 1823, shortly after Liholiho's departure for England, a town crier "ordered the people not to work, travel or even light fires on the Sabbath and the orders were repeated on the other islands" (Daws, 72). Soon the word went forth ordering the natives to attend school and observe the Sabbath by attending the new church. Among other pleasures denied by church and state were Sunday horseback riding and playing music. Playing billiards at any time was seriously frowned upon.

Clearly the laws she set forth were taken from the Bible as the missionaries interpreted it, and were enforced. A moral tone for the kingdom was set and the natives were expected to fall in line. "For six years since her baptism Ka'ahumanu had sought to make God's law the foundation for the law of the land" (Silverman, 130).

It was in this Puritan atmosphere that three Roman Catholic priests and three Catholic lay brothers arrived in Honolulu in July 1827.

CHAPTER FOUR

Arrival of Catholic Priests

Joining the royal group that accompanied King Kamehameha II to England was the young Frenchman Jean Baptiste Rives, who traveled as the king's secretary and interpreter. Rives had long lived in Hawai'i and owned extensive lands on O'ahu, Moloka'i and Hawai'i Island (Day *Biographical*, 109). The titles to some of these lands were questionable and later would make him persona non grata with Ka'ahumanu and ruling chiefs.

Leaving London after the demise of Liholiho and Kamāmalu, Rives went to his homeland. He had two goals. One was to form a mercantile business in the Sandwich Islands that would benefit not only the traders but himself as well. He found interested business-related individuals who formed what was planned to become a French colony in Oceania. He also was seeking the establishment of a Catholic mission in the Islands.

He met with enthusiasm from French church officials, especially the newly formed order of the Congregation of the Sacred Hearts of Jesus and Mary who saw this as an opportunity for its priests and lay brothers to spread their faith. After they received support from Parisian ecclesiastics in March 1825, the matter was referred to Rome for papal approval. Pope Leo XII granted it.

Cheered by this support, a mission group of three priests and three brothers was formed. Father Alexis Bachelot was chosen to be the apostolic prelate in Oceania. Before departing Bordeaux in November 1826 (after months of delays and false starts), Rives assured Bachelot that he personally would be in Honolulu to receive them and pave the way for their establishment. Rives had already made light of the fact that Protestantism in Hawai'i would be a problem. Both assurances turned out to be false.

But it would be nine long months on the ship *La Comete* before they would arrive at their destination. After a stop in Brazil, they passed through the hazardous Straits of Magellan. Three weeks later they anchored off the port of Valparaiso where they were welcomed and hosted at the convent of the Franciscan friars. After a two-week sojourn, with some recovering from unceasing bouts of seasickness, they debarked for Honolulu, a trip which included stops at Callao in Peru and Mazatlan in Mexico.

> On July the 6th about noon, they sighted the snow-capped summit of Mauna Kea piercing the clouds which kept most of the island hidden from their eyes. Having left Maui and Moloka'i to the Southwest, they were near O'ahu early on the morning of the seventh. Father Bachelot said Mass at seven o'clock to ask God's blessing over the mission they were about to establish. Soon Diamond Head was cleared, and about ten o'clock, La Comete cast anchor in Honolulu. They were fully prepared for an unfavorable reception.
>
> (Yzendoorn, 33)

When they arrived on July 7, 1827, it had been almost nine months since they left Bordeaux. Unknown to them as they touched the Sandwich Islands for the first time, Ka'ahumanu had issued a decree which denied vessels the right to debark any persons not approved by the throne. But *La Comete* was not challenged at the port and it appears that their entry was not openly opposed. It was in this sort of a nebulous atmosphere that the French found themselves.

But where was Rives, with his promise of paving the way and thus lessening the likelihood of holy competition? The entrepreneur was nowhere to be seen. Nor would he ever be seen in Hawai'i again. Shortly after the six missionaries finally departed from Bordeaux, Rives learned through a ship's captain that if he ever returned to the Islands he would face serious trouble with the powers that be. He was accused not only of stealing large sums of money from Liholiho during the London visit but even of stealing the dead king's valuable watch! His reputation, cloudy at best with some of the chiefs and the queen regent herself, led to the confiscation of his many lands. His honor thus sullied, Rives never returned to the islands where he was now unwelcome.

Rives instead chose to enter into business in California. He later moved to Mexico where he died in August 1833, at the age of forty. Left behind were his Hawaiian wife and children. To his credit, Rives had written Father Bachelot in Honolulu apologizing for his failure to appear upon the priests' arrival.

The three priests were eager to establish themselves. Heading the group with Father Bachelot were Fathers Patrick Short (from Ireland) and Abraham Armand. Three lay brothers, Theodore Boissier, Melchior Bondu and Leonard Portal, also accompanied them to establish Hawai'i's first Catholic mission. None of them could foresee the resistance they would meet over the next few years. Had Jean Rives accompanied them, his Hawaiian contacts perhaps would have smoothed the transition (31–32).

Accompanying the French missionaries on the sea voyage was a French lawyer, Philippe August de Morineau. The French government had earlier looked to him as the leader of a small

French colony in the village of Honolulu. It also hoped that he would be instrumental in the establishment of "missionaries and mechanics in the Hawaiian Islands." Along with the American consul, John Jones, de Morineau was responsible for procuring a small piece of land on which the French clerics could establish their mission, located on the site of the present-day Our Lady of Peace Cathedral in Central Honolulu. (The Fort Street edifice is said to be the oldest still-operating Catholic cathedral in the United States.)

Also helpful in obtaining land for the small mission band was O'ahu governor Boki. The British Consul General, Richard Charlton, in a document dated June 24, 1841, did "hereby certify that a certain piece or parcel of land situated in the town of Honolulu, and now occupied by the French mission was given by Boki, at that time governor of Oahu, to Mess. Bachelot and Short, but whether for their own private use, or use of the mission I do not know. I do further certify that the king Kamehameha the 3d. was present when it was given...and that Manula...was directed by Boki in the presence of the king to measure the aforesaid land" (38).

The enclosure for their future home was about forty yards square, or about a third of an acre. The three small grass huts served their immediate needs. One was a general room, described as a small parlor, that served as sleeping quarters at night. The second small room was a combined "cellar, garret, storeroom...and workshop." The remaining room was used as a chapel in the morning and in the evening. Otherwise it served as a study room.

And study they did, their work made more difficult due to the lack of a Hawaiian dictionary or grammar. A French ship's captain, on a visit to his countrymen, said, "When I visited them in their solitude, they were assiduously occupied with the study of native tongue, later to be able to exert resources far superior to those of their rivals." He also found them poorly lodged.

But their time spent inside was perhaps to their advantage since they did not wish to be conspicuous and draw undue attention to themselves for the present. They knew they needed to learn the Hawaiian tongue and dedicated the first few weeks to that purpose.

Their visitors were at first few, but some natives and an occasional foreigner found their way to the mission out of curiosity or a desire to be hospitable. But generally the missionaries wanted to lay low, to remain inconspicuous. "In the beginning they seldom left their dwelling, confident that if they kept out of the public eye initially, the chiefs and people would become familiar with occasional sightings of the French priests, and their animosity having cooled down, would tolerate their presence" (35).

But the number of friendly visitors increased, sometimes more than the priests cared to have. Some of them dared to attend the morning Mass, or showed up for evening services. Soon the numbers increased to the extent that "...their huts were thronged with visitors...some times with chiefs, the latter never coming without a train. They come in, squat down, speak partly by signs, partly in their language, look at us and contemplate us with ease and finally leave as they had come" (36).

About two weeks after their arrival, the priests were summoned to appear before Ka'ahumanu, the queen regent herself. Assuming the dowager's dark purpose, "and not wishing to expose themselves to a formal order to depart they prudently neglected to answer the call" (36).

In hindsight one might ask if indeed that was the prudent response, considering the position of the queen and the potential to perhaps defuse any hostility. Soon after, Captain La Plassard of *La Comete* was called before the queen, and he did go. There he was told by Ka'ahumanu to "re-embark the priests." He refused, inasmuch as he was still owed for their passage from France. When the day of debarkation for the vessel drew near, the queen sent for Boki. She expected the governor of O'ahu to put them aboard forcibly. Fortunately for the priests, Boki was thirty miles away and the French ship sailed two hours before his return. It is doubtful that Boki would have been at all cooperative considering his Catholic ties, such as they were. He was known to be friendly to the priests since he approved the transaction making available to them the land they occupied.

A few days later, the long-established Don Francisco de Paula Marin visited the priests and informed them that one of the Protestant ministers had asked him to make introduction to the recently arrived Catholics. Marin refused, for reasons of his own, and suggested that the minister go by himself, assuring him he would be well-received. Initially the Protestant clergymen had expected a call from the newcomers. They had repeatedly stated they would be pleased to receive the Catholics, saying that there was work enough for all. However, it was Father Bachelot's opinion that no good either for the priests' undertaking or for themselves would come from such friendly intercourse and, "he thought it prudent to remain at home" (37). Once more, "prudence" rather than Christian courtesy was the order of the day for the new arrivals.

In a letter to his superiors in Paris, Bachelot describes a visit from the Protestant missionary.

Anyhow, one of these gentlemen, not finding Mr. Marin to introduce him...paid us a preparatory visit and after two days introduced the missionary. As we did not wish to consider this call as made to us at all, Mr. [Father] Patrick, being a Britisher, received it alone...mention was made of religion, and the minister was kind enough to admit that there are honest people in all religions, and especially among Catholics; he invited Mr. Patrick to call on the Protestant missionaries and wanted to take him along for that purpose...Father Patrick did go two days later, but simply to return the call of the minister...The latter received him very amiably, and introduced his colleagues. He received a call of another minister two days later, but did not think it necessary to repay the visit.

(Yzendoorn, 37)

Apparently Bachelot sent Father Patrick as an emissary instead of going himself.

Shortly after, records Yzendoorn, the Protestant ministers offered Brother Melchior a job working in their printing shop. Brother Melchior declined the job "from reasons of Conscience," out of prudence, perhaps. But was this not still another missed opportunity to work in the field side by side with other Christians?

An astute observer and chronicler of the times was the captain of the French ship *Heros*, Auguste Bernard Duhaut-Cilly. The vessel traveled frequently between California and the Sandwich Islands. Duhaut-Cilly wrote much more than a journal. His work was published in Paris in 1834 under the title of *Autour du monde, principalement à la California et aux Îles Sandwich*. It was published in two volumes.

His descriptions of the Hawaiian culture, landscape, towns and villages, customs and habits reveal the impressions of a talented writer who often went into great detail in describing his settings and opinions. For instance, when he visited the domicile of the French priests he "found them living in wretched conditions although they seemed to bear their hardships cheerfully and with courage. They related to me all the difficulties they had encountered when seeking admission to the islands..." They told Duhaut-Cilly of the threat of expulsion from the islands that hung over their heads.

"Before leaving France," wrote Duhaut-Cilly, "I had clearly anticipated that these clerical gentlemen would not be received in the islands without strong objection. I was also quite aware that...for several years Protestant missionaries had been established in the Sandwich Islands and were enjoying the good graces of the elderly Kaou-Manou [Ka'ahumanu]; but I was ignorant of the degree of credence and influence they had attained. So well had they understood how to dominate this woman that now she sees only through their eyes and acts only on their instigation. Therefore it was but natural to suppose that they would not put envy aside and allow missionaries of the Catholic faith to land in the islands" (Korn, 20).

After referring to "the power of the Protestant missionaries," he credits them not only with introducing the Christian faith to the islands but also teaching Hawaiians to read and write and bringing them the moral meaning of the Gospel. "They even operate a printing press with which they are able to transcribe and publish in the language of the country such works of writing as they deem suitable for placing in native hands" (ibid.).

But the captain deplores what he sees as the abandonment of agriculture to the extent "that the life of the people has deteriorated and rapidly declined, and indeed has diminished as much as a third."

He blames the missionaries for this in that "women and children, old folks and adults, all have been forced to submit to learning their lessons and to devote any day and all day to doing so, while leaving their fields untilled and their traditional plantations...to be devoured by noxious weeds."

Nor is Duhaut-Cilly at all happy with the adult population being compelled to help build churches, attend religious services and otherwise obey the wishes the queen regent whose bowing to the missionaries dominated the lives of the people. Observed the captain,

We ourselves witnessed some of the cruelties practiced by the American missionaries under the mask of religion...I was shown a young woman of eighteen whose neck, body, and limbs were furrowed with scars from her having been clapped in irons. Her crime, I was informed, was that she had fled from a husband supplied her by the Methodists. What an offense! That a poor woman who had never a notion of what marriage is except what she had acquired from her father and mother—in other words to remain "faithful" just so long as it suited her to remain so and no longer.

Duhaut-Cilly was an inquisitive man, so much so that he arranged inland trips to such far-off O'ahu places as the village of Waialua on the north shore of the island. But his highest praise goes to the native Hawaiians. He found the men to be handsome, the women beautiful and all blessed with an outgoing warmth of hospitality and charm. "Ready to be amused by the least trifle, their lips never fail to smile. Neither does the mouth open to utter a refusal. It is therefore not astonishing that a foreigner, having experienced so hospitable and easy a welcome among them, should give way under the influence of such behavior" (Korn, 16).

These sentiments had also been expressed earlier by the three French priests.

CHAPTER FIVE

The Persecutions Begin

It was in early April of 1828 that the second company of New England missionaries arrived to reinforce their brethren. It was also then that the Protestant Mission formed a committee to look into the operations and details and plans of what they mistakenly called the "Jesuits." (The priests were not Jesuits. They were members of the Sacred Hearts Fathers.) Heading the fact-finding committee was the Reverend Hiram Bingham, the acknowledged leader of the Mission, assisted by Levi Chamberlain and E. W. Clark. The long and short of their work was to declare that these Papist interlopers would have to go "because their teachings were immoral and dangerous to the State" (Yzendoorn, 44).

Their findings, which they refer to as "specimens" of false teachings practiced by Catholics, alleged and focused on, among other things, Catholic worship of idols and false images. Here Yzendoorn makes it clear to the reader that "Catholics never pray *to*, but often pray *before* images...it is only a difference of prepositions; but in theology grammatical blunders are far reaching" (45).

In its final statement, in January 1830, to the General Meeting of the Mission, "The committee would earnestly recommend to the meeting to determine upon a course, which the Mission as a body and as individuals should pursue in relation to this dangerous sect."

On January 21, the overall committee submitted nine resolutions after a lengthy "Whereas." The resolutions are summarized except for direct quotations:

1. The Jesuits are imposing their doctrines on "this ignorant people. They are dangerous to the civil government of these islands, they are hinderers of the progress of the people in civilization and in literature. They are enemies of morality and of the Religion of Jesus Christ."

2. The mission should recognize that "every man for his religious beliefs and practices, when not leading to immorality, is accountable only to God and his own conscience...all coercive measures of civil authority to control religious opinions and practices, except as above noted, are improper and injurious."

3. The civil government has the right to send away any foreign resident without assigning the reason.

4. The government has the right to punish transgressors of the law, foreigners and natives alike. Any person inducing others to violate the law shall be liable to penalty.

5. It is not persecution when the Chiefs ask our opinion or advice, fairly to tell them that the Jesuits as a body are dangerous to the civil, moral and religious prosperity of the islands. The Chiefs should not inflict punishment on them on account of their religion, but only if they break the civil laws.

6. There is a duty to make known to the Chiefs historical facts regarding the practices and principles of the Jesuits.

7. It is proper to teach the people of Honolulu from the pulpit on this subject. The committee recommends that the subject be treated on the other islands, not to point out the Jesuits except by inference and say nothing respecting them except in private.
8. The committee should inform the Chiefs that if they do plan to send the Jesuits away or do not consent to their staying, they cannot prohibit their preaching or proselytizing ...without taking away the right of conscience from them, and thus subjecting religious opinions to the law of the land.
9. Considering that the mission has such enemies in their midst "should lead us to make greater exertions to teach the people to read, think and reflect...on the grand system of religion."

(Yzendoorn, 46–47).

Resolution Six stands out for the opportunity the missionaries give themselves by instructing the chiefs in the matter of the "Jesuits." Today it would be called an opportunity for brainwashing.

The Protestant Mission provided the teachers and the textbooks for native students attending so-called public schools. The books were, for the most part, printed on the Mission press in Honolulu. In 1832 it printed "A Geography—something describing the form of the earth, and things on it." The "things on it" included a description of the "ignorance and deceitful and lying teachers of the pope." Geography it was not, but it was a very useful medium in reaching the minds of the native students. The English translation follows:

The French people who dwell there [Canada] are very ignorant. Many of them do not know the palapala (books).

When they came to Canada they came with bad teachers. They were lying teachers who followed the religion of the Pope. They were deceitful teachers. They did not teach the people the palapala, lest their wickedness and deceit should be known. They taught the people to assent to the words of the priest only. They said to them that they would repent for the sins of the people. It was good for them that the people should remain in their sins, and that the heart should fear death. Then by paying a large sum of money to the priest he would repent for them. The priests would not repent for the sins of any man who had little money. But if the sum was large then all was well; though he was a murderer, a thief, or a rebel, the priests repented and appeased GOD. It was a constant practice with the people to confess their sins to the priest, paying him, when the instructor would say it is well. Then the man was at rest, believed the sins truly remitted by the priest, and, that in him his soul lived.

Many persons in the United States went to dwell in Canada, some English also. They practiced goodness there. They did not assent to follow deceitful teachers, avaricious persons. They promulgated the word of GOD, exposed the wickedness of the priests, and showed what is good for man and what gives life.

The priests constituted masters of countries, and exalted themselves above the word of GOD. They also elected some one and made him appear superior to Jesus Christ on earth. He is called the Pope.

He (the Pope) lives in great pomp, believing himself to be equal to GOD. To him it belongs to pardon men's sins, to him to give salvation. The man who pays him the most money will attain it.

A very great number of men followed him (the Pope) in past times. Some forsook him, but many remain with him at this time. Many in France, in Spain, and in other countries act in like manner. His word is very powerful. If a man prays according to the word of GOD as we do, he is punished with death; very many have been murdered there, the number is countless

(HMP, 65)

Such was the geography of the world, Hawaiian Mission version. While resolutions had been passed at the 1830 General Meeting of the missionaries, not all favored the recommendations. As Bingham himself wrote:

About this time Governor Adams (Kuakini) was encouraged by one of our missionaries to believe that no effort ought to be made by the government to restrain or send away the Catholic missionaries, but just to leave them to the disposal of Providence, to go or to stay, to preach, to proselyte or to refrain. When Kuakini mentioned this to another missionary, he objected and said he thought the sovereign had a right to deny them a residence in the kingdom, as they were unwelcome or dangerous to the state. Of course he was, on the "disagreement of the doctors" or novices, left to decide for himself on the merits of the question.

(Bingham *Report*, in Yzendoorn, 49)

Most of the missionaries at the General Meeting were from the other Hawaiian islands and came annually to Honolulu for that purpose. It may be inferred that all active opposition to the Catholics "was concentrated in the sturdy and unbending Mr. Bingham to whose influence the majority of the ministers had yielded" (49).

The Boston missionaries were not alone in their efforts to prejudice the chiefs against the Catholic intrusion. A Captain

Dale, of the ship *Fawn*, presumably British, made it his business to inform the young King Kamehameha III that there had been at one time a great slaughter of his ancestors in England by the Catholics and that "If Roman Catholics gain much influence here, you may expect your islands to be filled with blood..."

Another party whose country lacked neutrality was Captain W. C. B. Finch of the U.S. ship of war *Vincennes*, which had dropped anchor in Honolulu harbor October 13, 1829. He was the bearer of a letter from the U.S. Secretary of the Navy, said to be written by the direction of the President. It was directed to the young king, congratulating him on "the rapid progress which had been made by his people in acquiring the knowledge of letters and of the true religion—the religion of the Christian Bible" (*Suppliment,* 11–12). The chief aim of this visit, says Yzendoorn, "seems to have been to strengthen the hands of the American missionaries, which effect was fully attained. The chiefs were exultant" (Yzendoorn, 51).

Some American traders and merchants were indifferent as to whether Catholics should be allowed, but, afraid of French competition in matters of trade, they may have told the chiefs about the reputed bloody character of those Romanists. Ka'ahumanu, says Yzendoorn, "thanks perhaps to the oft repeated infusions of energy by Rev. Bingham, was alone among all the chiefs, ready to take action against the French. Her hands were tied by Boki, who would fain have snatched the regency from her" (50). Relations between the two were just shy of open hostility. As governor of Oahu, Boki had his share of supporters, and Ka'ahumanu knew it. Though they were cousins, no love was lost between them. And Boki, a baptized Catholic, had authorized acquisition of the property the priests now lived upon and thus had showed his favoritism to the Catholics.

But on August 8, 1830, at Bingham's residence, with the two adversaries present, Ka'ahumanu "prevailed upon Boki to take steps to arrest the progress of the Catholic religion" (ibid.).

Boki, not daring to refuse her pressing requests, issued a proclamation, carried by the town crier to the village streets, prohibiting all natives from attending services of the Catholic priests. Violators would be punished by being exiled or even being thrown into a canoe and set adrift in the ocean.

Bachelot wrote a letter to the head of his Paris religious order on August 19, 1829 in which he reported that, "On pain of being deprived of their belongings, having their house burnt, being put in prison, and chastised with rods" (50), the neophytes still were undeterred. He cited the case of one Luika (Louise) who had been born and baptized in the Mariana Islands, probably Guam. Ka'ahumanu personally ordered her to attend the Protestant services, something Luika refused to do. She would ultimately pay for her recalcitrance by being exiled to Maui, there to be in the service of a strict Protestant householder.

About this time Boki, an entrepreneur of sorts who owned a store and a hotel, sought to repay some of his debts to Honolulu merchants, and to increase his personal wealth, by sailing to the far-off New Hebrides to gather the prized and valuable sandalwood. Boki outfitted a ship, the *Kamehameha*, that he commanded, and sailed with more than 250 men. A companion ship, the *Becket*, had a like number of adventurers and crew. A year or more later, the *Becket* returned to Honolulu, with only a small handful of its original crew, the rest having died of disease. As for the *Kamehameha*, it was never heard from again. One theory is that members of the crew were careless in smoking and somehow the great amount of powder on the vessel was ignited, destroying the ship and all its crew, including Boki. It was also said that the vessel was lost in a storm or wrecked on a reef in uncharted waters.

Once it was determined, months later, that Boki was lost at sea, Boki's wife, Liliha, who had acted as governess of O'ahu in his absence, was deposed by Ka'ahumanu, along with her supporters. Ka'ahumanu was now fully in charge and set about to enforce more vigorously the civil laws. These laws, which were established by the chiefs and the queen-regent, strictly prohibited the practice of Catholicism by native Hawaiians. (Foreigners were not affected.)

The chiefs, who had had the missionaries as their teachers, were faithful pupils. The Catholic priests and natives had lost their friend and protector, Boki. He would be missed. With no Boki to restrain Kaʻahumanu's "persecuting proclivities," the priests' chapel was invaded more than once and the neophytes ousted.

The previously mentioned Luika was incarcerated in the fort-prison, but a chief of Boki's party had her freed. Soon, however, she was arrested again, along with her uncle, Valeriano, and one Kimeone Pale. Conducted before the chiefs, they "were asked many questions, whilst blows were rained upon them during the entire interrogatory...when the bastinido proved ineffective they were allowed to go free" (53).

On January 2, 1830, the persecutions increased. Pulcheria, a Catholic native, had been put in the prison and was denied food for two days. On the third day, "tired of the importunities and threats of the chiefs and Protestant catechists, who did not cease terrifying her" (53), and fearing she would be dragged off to the Calvinist prayer meeting, she made her escape. Searchers sought her out at the priests' chapel. Not finding her there (where she had attended an early Mass), "the agents of Kaahumanu" drove out the other worshipers they found.

Shortly after this incident, Father Bachelot called on the queen to protest the violation of his domicile. Far from giving him satisfaction, Kaʻahumanu forbade him to teach the Catholic religion in any form, "to which the Prefect Apostolic firmly answered that he could not refuse instruction in the only true religion to those who asked for it" (54). The queen ratified the permission given earlier by Boki to reside in the islands. She allowed foreigners to practice their religion but prohibited natives to partake of services at the chapel.

That same day, January 3, 1830, the young king promulgated an order that all native Catholics must appear before him two days later. While many refused to comply, those who attended were informed by the king of his opposition to Catholicism. After he questioned the degree of their faith, and urged them to attend Calvinist services, several fell in line, aware of punishment previously inflicted on their companions. One renegade, Akeriniko, who later returned to the Catholic fold, was a forty-year-old man who had been instructed in the Catholic teachings by Luika. He had been baptized and soon became an ardent instructor to those interested in Catholicism, an act which soon found him fettered in irons and placed in the prison. Denied food, he was sometimes pitied by the guards who provided him with sustenance under cover of darkness. He drank water from the open well in the prison yard. Luika, who lived in a small house across from the prison, also slipped him food when she could. During this period, Akereniko gained his freedom. But only briefly, for a few months later he was captured and "again condemned to hard labor for the crime of Popery" (55).

When Ka'ahumanu was absent from Honolulu, often on visits to another part of O'ahu, or even to another island, she left in her place Kīna'u. The daughter of Kamehameha I, she was to become the mother of Kamehameha IV and Kamehameha V. She too was imbued with the same Calvinist vigor as the missionaries had imparted to Ka'ahumanu, maybe more. Father Bachelot called her "...our greatest enemy" (56). Historian A. Grove Day records that "Kinau succeeded the deceased Ka'ahumanu as kuhina-nui in 1832 and continued the policy of strictly enforcing laws inspired by missionary teachings" (Day *Biographical*, 78).

One who suffered for her faith under Kīna'u was the twenty-one-year-old widow, Alokia. Despite carrying a child at her breast, she and seven other Catholics were seized, "put into irons and made to appear before Kinau who tried in vain to shake their constancy" (57). In prison, she and the other captives were denied food. Her survival was due to the cleverness of Brother Melchior who smuggled food to the persecuted inmates. Yzendoorn reports that the prisoners "were next applied to hard labor; the men having to cut stones on the reef, the women to make a certain number of mats."

But Alokia grew ill, no doubt still suffering from the recent death of her husband as well as her ill-treatment in the prison. Nonetheless she was compelled to perform the hard labor. Her health deteriorated by fatigue and privations, though her burden was lightened by companions who charitably performed for her. One day her health was so poor the other prisoners had to carry her back to the jail on their shoulders. Says Yzendoorn, "The commandant of the fort was in secret friendly to us. Our Christians were well treated by him." However Alokia declined rapidly. Learning of her impending death, Bachelot went to the fort and gave her the last rites of the Catholic church. "Our Lord called her to her reward." Her baby was adopted by a Catholic woman. The author concluded by stating, "May this Holy Martyr who laid down her life for her faith, obtain for all her countrymen the grace to embrace it and practice it with the same generosity and firmness!" (58).

It is to the credit of the British consul Charlton that upon occasion he was able to provide prisoners with relief. Once when a petty chief was conducting some prisoners to their work place, they passed the residence of the consul. At that point, Esther, one of the group, complained, "It is already a long time that you have kept us at work without so much as giving us anything to eat. This foreigner here [Charlton] is kindly disposed, we are hungry and going inside." The guards tried to stop them but

Charlton, attracted by the "tumult" came out and drove the guards off, with verbal abuse. Charlton took the prisoners in, fed them and, according to Yzendoorn, gave them lodging for eight days (82).

But this was not to end the travail of that prisoner "gang." A few months later two of them, Ailimu and Pilipe died "as a consequence of the ill-treatments they had been exposed to." At one point two women, Kilika and Lahina, who refused to attend Bingham's services, were put in irons. They were "condemned to gather with their hands the excrement in a lane used by the prisoners of the fort as a place to satisfy their natural needs. During the night the hands of the poor sufferers were manacled but in the morning their fetters were taken off that they might work at their ignominious task...To their shame, the rabble frequently gathered in the lane, and followed the confessors with hoots and abuse when they carried their unseemly burdens to the sea" (89).

But despite the vicious nature of their punishment, the prisoners remained true to their faith, even inspiring others to learn more about Catholic teachings.

One catechist named Simeon, along with half a dozen others, was arrested after refusing to change his faith. The group was assigned, like the women, to carry filth from the cells to a place near the ocean. Simeon must have rankled his guards, for one morning Brother Melchior found him flat on a table, his neck, hands and feet attached with iron shackles.

Days later some of the Hawaiian "teachers" called on Simeon to learn whether his obstinacy had been cured. Finding him still resolute in the Catholic faith, they beat him and forced him to go to work despite his weakened physical condition. Two weeks later Simeon's wife, Marianne, was jailed for "popery" and "like her husband, had her neck and limbs encircled with gyves." Messengers were sent frequently to Simeon and Marianne by Kīna'u who sought in vain to shake their constancy. All she got from Simeon was the same answer: "If they demand me to do work of any kind, I will submit to it. But as to denying my faith, I cannot consent" (90). His wife gave the same answer.

At one point, several of the foreigners were so incensed at the treatment given the native Catholics that they carried their concerns to Kīna'u through the medium of the American consuls. They might have succeeded "had not Bingham opposed them, saying that all Hawaiians ought to be of one mind" (89).

The supplement to the *Sandwich Island Mirror* reported that "Kimeone Paele…was beaten in the most cruel manner, kicked, trampled and spit upon by the members of the Protestant church but more feelingly so by a Mr. John Ii, a native celebrated for his piety who sought every opportunity and devised every means in his power to augment the torture and suffering of this miserable man."

CHAPTER SIX

The Expulsion

With friend and protector Governor Boki well out of the picture, the screws were more forcibly applied to Catholic priests accused of lies, deceit and idol worship.

On April 2, 1831, both Fathers Bachelot and Short received a summons to appear at the Fort, where affairs of state were sometimes conducted. This day it was an assembly of the chiefs, a number of native teachers, other natives and several foreigners.

The king, being a minor, was not present. As usual Ka'ahumanu was in command. A huge tent covered the open area. The stage was set for an ominous event.

Upon the entrance of the two priests, both Ka'ahumanu and her brother, high chief Kuakini, rose and offered their chairs, perhaps the only chairs present. Then, once the priests were seated, and as if on cue, chief Kaikeoewa, governor of the island of Kaua'i, stepped forward and solemnly and without a word, presented a letter to the Apostolic Prefect. It was dated January 18, 1831, about three months earlier. It was, assumes Yzendoorn, probably composed at an earlier convocation or revival at Ka'awaloa in Kona where "the rulers had been brought to a suitable pitch of religious frenzy" (60).

Father Bachelot read the letter silently, then shared it with his colleague, Father Short. Its contents were direct. It could not have been more explicit. It read:

Where are you, priests who have come from France?

This is our decree for your banishment. Begone from this land. Dwell not upon these Hawaiian Islands, for your doctrine is at variance with the religion which we profess. And because of teaching your religion to the people of this land, some of us have turned to your sentiments. We are endeavoring to spread among the people the religion which we profess—this religion we plainly know to be true. This is what we earnestly desire.

When you arrived here, we did not invite you, But you came of your own accord. Therefore we send you away. Begone.

We allow three months to prepare for your departure, and if within that time you shall not have gone, your effects will be confiscated, and you will be destitute; and if you wait until the fourth month, and we see you delaying, then, you will be imprisoned, and we shall do unto you, as do the Governments of all nations to those who disregard their commands. So will we constantly do to you. (signed)

> Kauikeaouli
> Ka'ahumanu
> Kaikeoewa
> Hoapili
> Naihe
> Kuakini

The above translation from the Hawaiian is by Robert Wyllie, probably while he was serving as foreign minister after 1845 (Wyllie, 273, in Yzendoorn, 60). The composition of the letter smacks strongly of "foreign," i.e., missionary, origin.

Bachelot says that, after a long period for reflection, "that I might speak without excitement," he responded that they could not consent to abandon their mission. Promising to leave the Islands would have been the equivalent to renouncing it. "You say that my religion is not good. But not knowing it, how can you condemn it? Here I took occasion to reproach them for their ignorance and their obstinacy, because they had never been willing to listen to us...Do you not know that I am not of this world? I belong to God and all I have is His. I have come here possessing only my body and the Word of God which I wished to give you. You would not accept it...I do not fear depredation; if you wish to take my goods from my home, go and get them; these things are of this world. Neither do I fear your gyves. Put me in jail. God who sees and hears us, will be there with me" (61).

Chief Kuakini reminded the priests that they had arrived without permission. When Bachelot responded that they had been authorized by Governor Boki, he was reminded that Boki was dead and all he had done was now null and void.

Bachelot pressed the point that the chiefs ought not condemn the Catholic religion without first knowing it. To this Kuakini replied, "Perhaps you are right, but you are a stranger; our teacher [meaning Bingham] is likewise a stranger...He came first and taught us his religion, and we found it good and adopted it. If you had arrived first, we would have listened to you with the same docility, but you came last and it is not good that there should be two religions, for this would soon result in war" (63).

The answer to that, replied Bachelot, "was not who came first but who taught the truth." He described the separation of the Protestants from the Catholic Church three centuries earlier. He also discussed the Catholic doctrine of honoring the saints and their images, which, he said, was not like what the Protestant teachers made their people believe (ibid.).

Much discussion followed, but the central point was that the priests had come without being invited and now they had been given their marching orders. Brother Melchior was exempted from this edict, probably because he was a lay brother and not an ordained minister of the Catholic church. The die was cast.

Shortly after the meeting, a great many visitors came to the Catholic compound to express their sympathy. Among the callers was chief Kaikeoewa, who had delivered the letter at the meeting. Apparently embarrassed, he disclosed the purpose of his visit, saying, "I come to speak about what you know well, and upon which we have agreed together."

"I understand," answered Bachelot, "you come to drive me out."

"Not that, we do not drive you out; but it is expedient that you go quietly back to your country."

"How is that if you do not drive me away, why do you want me to go against my will? I have my disciples here; are they thieves, murderers or fornicators?"

"No, you are orderly and good, but it is better that you go."

Here Father Bachelot repeated what he had said at the assembly. The chief did not answer, but having been shown around the premises soon took leave with the utmost politeness (ibid.).

The two priests took pains to stall the three-month departure. Whenever a vessel was about to debark the priests applied in writing to the captain for free passage. The captains, knowing the intentions of the priests, and unwilling to be the executors of a decree of banishment, denied the requests. At one point, when the Prussian ship *Prinzessin Luiza* was in port, the governor of O'ahu went to Captain Wendt, urging him to take the two Catholic missionaries back to Europe. Captain Wendt agreed, but, well aware of the priests' desire to remain, said he must first be paid five thousand dollars. Wendt knew that this sum, exorbitant to the chiefs, could not be met. The vessel soon sailed off without the two clergymen. They had artfully managed a delay of banishment. The threat to confiscate their property after three months was not carried out.

Meanwhile, it was observed that a number of natives no longer attended Protestant prayer meetings as they had previously. This created a stir in the Calvinist camp. When twelve neophytes were arrested and questioned, they replied that they had joined the Catholic religion, they wished to preserve it and were willing to suffer any punishment that might be inflicted on them. Their "willingness" would be tested.

Ka'ahumanu condemned them to hard labor. Each one had to build a stone-wall fifty-feet long, six-feet high and three- to four-feet wide. They were forbidden to help one another in this task. The walls were to be erected at Waikīkī, then a dreary plain. The ground was covered with stones, many embedded in the ground. Having no tools of any kind, the prisoners were left to use their hands as best they could (68).

It was Yzendoorn's feeling, many years later, that these prisoners (confessors of their faith he called them), "deserve to have their names recorded as on a roll of honor." They were, as he recorded the names:

Pelipe Mokuhou, aged 50
Kikime Kaihekauila, aged 28
Pakileo Luakini, aged 24
Nanekea Nanauwahi, aged 70
Kekilia Kakau, aged 50
Monika Ai, aged 50
Aika Kapuloaokalani, aged 60
Amelia Uheke, aged 50
Akaka Kamoohula, aged 36
Helena Keehana, aged 50
Mahaoi
Ailimu (ibid.)

The prisoner Amelia Uheke (Esther) was a chiefess from Kaua'i. She had been caught reading a pamphlet given her by Bachelot, titled "Exposition of the Catholic Doctrine." She was arrested and summoned before a chief who ordered her to attend Protestant services, threatening her with hard labor should she refuse. Refuse she did, and despite her rank, accepted her punishment "rather than to deny her religion."

The Catholics were about equally divided between males and females. Ailimu had a six-year-old child who accompanied her in imprisonment (68). Kikime, a male, was blind, and he alone was permitted to work alongside his mother, Monika Ai. The mother located the stones, and the son, following her directions, dug them up and, together, they carried them to pile them up for the wall. The first few days the prisoners had fetters on their ankles and wrists, but these were removed shortly.

Another prisoner, Aneroniko, who had escaped from the prison-fort four months earlier, was arrested and made to join the work gang "with his coreligionists."

Food was a problem. It was provided sparingly and relatives and friends were prohibited from bringing it in. Nonetheless they did so, often with the help of a compassionate guard. The author writes of the prisoners, "they appeared blithe...because, as they said, they suffered for God and not for having committed any crime" (*Annals*, 114, in Yzendoorn, 68).

Meanwhile, the government was no longer waiting for a friendly vessel to transport the priests from the kingdom. It had plans of its own to outfit the small vessel *Waverley* which was government property. It took some time to find a master for the ship but, eventually, the chiefs persuaded an Englishman, Captain Sumner, to take command. Despite remonstrances from sympathetic foreigners against Sumner for accepting this assignment, there were no hard feelings on the part of Bachelot. Sumner, an aging and unemployed seaman, had a family to provide for. Said Bachelot, "The principal crime of that unfortunate man was his wish to gain a living and nourishment for his children" (69).

On November 5, 1831, Captain Sumner received a commission, signed by the young king (under Ka'ahumanu's direction, if not with Bingham's input) which read:

> I, Kauikeaouli, King of the Sandwich Islands, and Kaahumanu and Kuakini, Governor of Oahu, do hereby commission William Sumner, commander of the brig Waverley, to receive on board two French gentlemen and their goods, or whatever they may bring on board, and to proceed on to California, and land them safe on shore, with everything belonging to them, where they may subsist, and then return back to the Sandwich Islands.
>
> (Wyllie, 274, in Yzendoorn, 69)

The priests learned of their pending deportation only by rumor, but not having been officially informed, they bided their time. Meanwhile, native Catholics often stopped by to worship or just visit the chapel.

By December 1837, the prisoners building the Waikīkī walls had been at their task for five months. One of the chiefs came and asked them if they were ready to embrace the teachings of Calvin at the Protestant church. When they declined they were visited by Bingham who hoped to provide them with appropriate Calvinist reading material. His description of his visit to the prisoners reads:

> About this time, but before the papal priests were sent away, I called at a little cluster of huts, where I found several of their followers sojourned, being employed daily in building a stone fence between the dry plain and the plantations at the rear, along between Punchbowl Hill and

Waikiki. Many hundreds of the people were from time to time, called out to work on this wall, on which the chiefs labored with their own hands. But this was the ordinary mode of executing public works: the other was special, and though I saw and heard neither chains, whips, nor instruments of torture, it was regarded as punishment. This was the only instrument of punishment which I ever saw inflicted on Hawaiian subjects who claimed to be papists. I asked Kaahumanu by what authority they were made to labor there. She said "by the law against idolatry; for they have violated the law in renewing the worship of images."

(Bingham *Residence*, 421, in Yzendoorn, 70)

It is hard to believe that the Reverend Bingham was so engaged in spreading the Good Word that he did not know for more than a year about the punishment that was being dealt out at the fort and the environs of the village.

Subsequently the "papists" were condemned to new and more severe punishments "from which they were to be delivered only about a year later by the combined and reiterated efforts of the reverend gentlemen who made up the Fifth Company of the Protestant missionaries who arrived on May 19, 1832. Also with the help of the British Consul, and that of Commodore Downes of the U.S. frigate Potomac" (70).

In early December 1831, the government issued its manifesto giving its reasons for expelling the priests. It read:

This is our reason for sending away the Palani [French]. In the first place, the chiefs never assented to their dwelling at Oahu; and when they turned some of our people to stand opposed to us, then we said, "Return to your own country whence ye came." At seven different times we gave them that order. And again, in speaking to them, we said, "Go away, ye Palani. We allow you three months to get ready."

But they did not go during the three months, but remained eight months, saying, "We have no vessel to return in." Therefore we put them on board our own vessel to carry them to a place where their service is like their own. Because their doings are different from ours and because we cannot agree, therefore we send away these men.

(Bingham Residence, 419, in Yzendoorn, 70)

A couple days after the issue of this order, Kīna'u's husband, high chief Kekūanaōa, informed the priests: "You could not go away because you pretended you had no vessel; there is one now; the day I come back you will depart" (70–71). Learning they would be welcomed at California missions the priests readied themselves for the day of departure, forced though it was.

Father Patrick Short, being a British subject, applied for the intervention of British consul Charlton. Charlton's appeal and protests to the government resulted in a dispatch from Ka'ahumanu which in effect told him to mind his own business.

Kind regards to you, British Consul. I make known to you in answer to your inquiries respecting the cause of complaint against these two men; it is on account of division and opposition, that I did not assent to these two men residing here. At first, I ordered them to return. I again ordered them away. They said, we have no vessel. Here is a vessel. I send them to another country. Do you be still. This business is ours, and that of my Protege adopted. Our vessel shall not treat them ill, but convey them safely. Some time to come, we then may write to the King of Great Britain. Such are our wishes. I forward this letter to you, that you may consider these things, and not act in haste, that trouble come not hereafter.

Kauikeaouli,

Kaahumanu (Wyllie, 274, in Yzendoorn, 71)

Meanwhile, the Catholic natives were not averse to visiting their pastors, often under cover of night, when the door of the little chapel was left open. Not only did they come to visit the priests but also the Blessed Sacrament. "Then they would say 'Ke Akua ka mua' (God before all)" (72).

At the request of the Prefect Apostolic, Bachelot and the American consul and the British consul provided written testimony to the good behavior of the priests. Charlton's declaration of support read:

> Woahoo, Sandwich Islands
> December 23, 1831.
>
> This is to certify that Mr. J. A. A. Bachelot and Mr. Patrick Short, who have resided at this Island ever since the year 1827 and who now are about to be sent away by the Chiefs, have during their residence here conducted themselves with the utmost propriety both to the Natives and Foreigners.
>
> I do also declare that Kaahumanu, the Queen Dowager and Regent of these Islands, declared unto me that they had been guilty of no crime but was [sic] sent away because they were Roman Catholics.
>
> Richard Charlton
> H.B.H. Consul
> (Archives, V. D. 4, in Yzendoorn, 73)

☩ ☩ ☩

The American Consul had much more to say on behalf of the Catholic clergymen.

> United States Consulate
> Sandwich Islands
>
> To all whom this may come. Be it known, that I, John C. Jones, Consul for the United States at the Sandwich Islands,

do publish and make known to the world that J. A. A. Bachelot and P. Short during a residence at the Sandwich Islands of four years, have always and at all times conducted themselves with the greatest propriety and decorum, obeying at all times the Laws and Regulations of these Islands, leading quiet and peaceful lives, respected by all foreigners who have had the pleasure to be made acquainted with them.

They have been persecuted and driven by force from these Islands to seek an asylum they know not where merely because they were Catholicks [sic], the King and Chiefs have publicly acknowledged, they have not a single charge against them; that their conduct has been meritorious and praiseworthy during their residence in these Islands, but because their religion is Catholick [sic], they have driven them from their shores.

Given under my hand and the seal of this Consulate at Oahu this Twenty fourth day of December, 1831.

John C. Jones
U.S. Consul
(Archives, V. D. 5, in Yzendoorn, 73)

Copies of both documents are in the archives of the Catholic Diocese of Honolulu.

The morning of that same day the priests celebrated Holy Mass at the chapel, Brother Melchior and an old Spaniard named Sobradello receiving the Holy Eucharist. Shortly after the service, about nine o'clock, Kekūanaō'a showed up to tell the priests, "Well, the time for departure has come."

"You want then to expel us by force?" asked Bachelot.

"Yes," he replied, laying his hands on Father Bachelot's shoulder (73).

Taking only their breviaries and their walking sticks, the two priests left the compound. Natives and foreigners alike climbed the fences of Fort Street to let them pass. Some seemed to rejoice. All the rest looked dismayed.

The march to the harbor was led by Kekūanaō'a, accompanied by a soldier of the government beating a drum. One who accompanied the priests was a foreigner and a Protestant, who had always shown himself attached to the pair. They were followed by a chief who was "ten steps behind, busy keeping the crowd at bay. On the way towards the harbor other foreign residents came to meet the exiles to express their sympathy and bid them farewell" (72).

It is worth mentioning at this point that the French historian Theodore Adolphe Barrot had high praise for the conduct of the two priests during their time in Honolulu. Yet Barrot was obviously not present at the time of their expulsion. Otherwise, he would not have written in his narrative *Unless Haste is Made* that "the two missionaries were dragged from their residence...and put on a vessel." This is quite contrary to the facts as described above.

At the harbor landing, Bachelot turned to his followers, who made up much of the procession. His address to them, translated later by a woman catechumen, Maria Leahi, said:

> It is not the chiefs of this country that wrong me; they are the victims of error and calumny. This is why they did not embrace the full religion. As for you, the mustard seed of the Gospel has been sown among you; I hope that it will bear fruits. Whilst you are without a priest, do not fail to pray as I have taught you. Beware of eating the bread of sacrilege in partaking of the Lord's supper with the Calvinists.

> (Archives, M. 25, in Yzendoorn, 74)

Why did Bachelot not appeal to his own government about the treatment French subjects had received from the kingdom of Hawai'i? Perhaps they feared that they might not have been believed, or that in the wake of the revolution which rocked France that July, no help would have been offered to them.

The two priests were carried by a small boat to the *Waverley* which lay along Robinson's dock. The captain was waiting for the arrival of the priests' baggage. It would have remained at the Catholic Mission had not British consul Charlton warned Kekūanaō'a that "if as little as a pin belonging to the priests remained ashore, trouble would be brewing for him" (74).

The baggage arrived in short order. Also a letter from the American consul, Jones, regretting his inability to see them off. An Irish sea-captain gave them a gift of a cask of Columbia River salmon. With no further delay the anchor was weighed and with the sails set, the brig cleared Honolulu harbor, headed for some point in California known only to the captain.

As for who was responsible for the actual expulsion, there was plenty of blame to go around. Was it Kekūanaō'a, he who enforced the expulsion? Or was it collectively the chiefs, that decision-making body who often took the advice of the missionaries? As for Ka'ahumanu, in a statement to Luika (Louise), she absolved herself. "I did not banish them," the queen said. "Bingham did."

"Bingham told you to banish them," rejoined Luika, "but you listened to him and ordered that they should be taken away on a vessel. If you had been unwilling, you would have closed your ears to the reasoning of Bingham, and our Fathers would be tranquilly here yet, as they used to be."

"Bingham is my light," said Ka'ahumanu, "He advised me to do it." Here the conversation ended (Yzendoorn, 80).

CHAPTER SEVEN

Exiled

The first day at sea was December 25, 1831, but Bachelot makes no mention of Christmas Mass being celebrated aboard the vessel.

It was, for the first few days, an unfriendly sea. It was listless, and, without wind, the *Waverley* lingered for most of the week before the outline of the Sandwich Islands disappeared. Nearly a month would pass before the mountains of California finally rose into view and the ship dropped anchor. It would be after they sailed by Catalina Island and hove into San Pedro Bay. They were, with their few belongings, rowed to shore and deposited on an uninhabited and inhospitable beach.

It had been the understanding of the priests that they would be dropped off at Santa Barbara or Monterey Bay, where there were friendly missions to welcome them, provide for them and use their services. But the penurious Captain Sumner, wishing to avoid anchorage fees at either place, sought the barren coast in between to discharge his two one-way travelers.

Fortunately, a farmer on horseback arrived at the scene, providing a potential link to the San Gabriel Mission, thirty miles away. Left by Sumner without food, they enjoyed a little cake which the farmer offered. Two bottles of water came from

The baptism of high chief Kalanimoku aboard the French ship *L'Uranie* off the Island of Hawai'i in 1819 is believed to be the first Catholic baptism in Hawai'i. (Hawai'i State Archives)

Liholiho, who was to become Kamehameha II, attended the baptism of Kalanimoku along with Ka'ahumanu. (Hawai'i State Archives)

Abbe de Quelen baptized Kalanimoku aboard the French vessel L'Uranie *that arrived in 1819, four months after the death of Kamehameha the Great. (Hawai'i State Archives)*

Ka'ahumanu, wife of Kamehameha I, and later kuhina nui (regent) of the Hawaiian Kingdom during the reigns of Kamehameha II and Kamehameha III, was instrumental in overthrowing the ancient kapu system in 1819. (Hawai'i State Archives)

Governor Boki (with his wife Liliha), younger brother of Kalanimoku, and governor of O'ahu, was baptized by Father de Quelen when the L'Uranie sailed to Honolulu. (Hawai'i State Archives)

Based on accounts by Native Hawaiians, William Ellis (seen here preaching), an early English missionary and historian, identified the kahuna Paʻao as a Roman Catholic priest. (Hawaiʻi State Archives)

In the 1820s, Kamehameha II and Kamehameha III lived in compounds which included not only traditional native houses, but structures of foreign influence. The first location of the royal compound was toward the rear of the village, near the home of the British Consul. Later, Hawaiian royalty moved closer to Kawaiahaʻo Church where the American Protestant mission was located. (Hawaiʻi State Archives)

STREET VIEW AT HONOLULU.

In this early 1830s scene of Honolulu (purportedly Fort Street), Levi Chamberlain, business agent of the Sandwich Islands Mission, is being pulled in a cart. (Bishop Museum)

Physician Thomas Holman, a non-ordained missionary, and his wife Lucia arrived on the Thaddeus *with the first group of Protestant missionaries. (Mission Houses Museum Library)*

Hiram Bingham, head of the first company of Protestant missionaries, was instrumental in Queen Kaʻahumanu's conversion to Christianity, and by extension, the entire Hawaiian nation's, after she pulled through an extensive illness. (Hawaiian Mission Children's Society Library)

At the age of eleven, Kauikeaouli (Kamehameha III, pictured here as an older man) succeeded the throne after Kamehameha II's death in 1824 from measles in England and came under the influence of Ka'ahumanu's Protestant inclinations. (Hawai'i State Archives)

Kawaiaha'o Church. (Hawaiian Mission Children's Society Library)

Princess Kina'u, kuhina nui after Ka'ahumanu's death, continued to support and promote the cause of Christianity. In this 1837 engraving by Masselot of the French frigate La Venus, *she is leaving First Bethel Church with her maids-of-honor. (Hawai'i State Archives)*

Cathedral of Our Lady of Peace located in central Honolulu, was built on land obtained by the first French clerics from Boki in 1841. (Archives, Diocese of Honolulu)

In 1831, Fathers Bachelot and Short were called to appear at Honolulu Fort before an assembly of chiefs, native teachers, and Ka'ahumanu, where they were presented with a letter "requesting" them to leave the islands. (Hawai'i State Archives)

Governor John Adams (High Chief Kuakini), brother of Ka'ahumanu, closed down grogshops and enforced the Sabbath laws for natives and foreigners alike. (Hawai'i State Archives)

In 1830, after complaining to Ka'ahumanu about an unauthorized search of his home, Father Bachelot was forbidden to teach the Catholic religion in any form. A church facility in Makiki was named after him. (Archives, Diocese of Honolulu)

Artist Guy Buffet's Lei of Bondage *painting (here reproduced in only one color) symbolizes the persecution heroically endured by the Hawaiians who embraced the Catholic faith. (Guy Buffet)*

Left: A practicing Catholic, Kimeone Paele (also known as Simeone) was beaten and trampled by members of the Protestant church for refusing to renounce the Catholic faith.

Center: Persecution of native Catholics included torture: Malia Makalena Kaha was tied to the rafters of a house, the thatches of which lacerated her face throughout her eighteen-hour ordeal.

Right: Like many Hawaiians who practiced Catholicism, Juliana Maku-wahine suffered persecution and torture under the strongly Protestant Native Hawaiian government which sought to stamp out Catholicism in the islands. (Reproductions of woodcuts in a Sandwich Islands Gazette *supplement)*

On July 21, 1837, a conference concerning the religious practices of Catholic fathers, Alexis Bachelot and Patrick Short, was held in a grass house adjoining the palace of King Kamehameha III, attended by the commanding officers of the French frigate, La Venus, *and the British warship,* Sulphur, *and the king himself. (Hawai'i State Archives)*

Rebuffed in his first attempt in 1837 to enter the islands, Desire (Louis) Maigret, later Bishop of the Sandwich Islands, traveled to Micronesia instead. (Archives, Diocese of Honolulu)

Captain Laplace of the French frigate, L'Artemise, *sailed to Hawai'i in 1839 with orders from King Louis Philippe to deliver a manifesto which addressed the treatment of French subjects and Catholics in particular. (Hawaiian Historical Society)*

Unimpressed by the missionaries, Kamehameha IV admired the Church of England, and asked Queen Victoria to send Anglican clergy to Hawai'i. (Hawai'i State Archives)

Queen Emma, wife of Kamehameha IV, was baptized into the Church of England by Bishop Staley. (Hawai'i State Archives)

In his Letters From the Sandwich Islands, *Samuel Clemens, then a writer for the* Sacramento Bee *referred to the Anglican Church as "a sort of nondescript wild cat religion imported here from England." (Hawai'i State Archives)*

One of the most successful missionary preachers, Reverend Titus Coan seen here with his wife Mrs. Fidelia Church Coan, are credited with converting over seven thousand natives. His congregation was one of the largest in the world. (Hawai'i State Archives)

Sumner, but nothing else except their baggage which the Hawaiian boatmen carried to the shore. Before departing, Sumner asked Bachelot for an "attestation of the good treatment they had received during the voyage, that he might show it to Kaahumanu" (76).

Probably with tongue in cheek, Bachelot gave him the following document:

> This is to certify that we the underwritten Catholic missionaries to the Sandwich Islands have been debarked with all our effects at a place called San Pedro, on the coast of California, and that we have been treated by Captain Sumner during our voyage with all the attention and interest we could have expected.
>
> 22 January, 1832.
J. A. A. Bachelot,
P. Short
(Yzendoorn, 76)

Thanks to two cowboys who learned, through the farmer, of the stranded passengers, the priests received a bottle of water and a bottle of milk. After a sleepless night on the beach the priests saw at dawn that the *Waverley* had sailed back toward Hawai'i. That day the farmer returned with a written message from the padre of a nearby community. Two hours later a carriage arrived and the party was on its way to San Gabriel. It was more than a day's travel so the priests spent the night at a ranch along the way. They were welcomed the next morning at the mission by the "joyous peals of bells, the happy faces of the villagers and the welcome of the good old Padre who told them they had finally found a home" (78).

While Father Short was to remain for some time at San Gabriel, he later went to the Mission San Juan Bautista, at least a day's journey away. In 1832, he was instrumental in founding a college in that region, said to be the first ever established in California (Bancroft III, 318, 777, in Yzendoorn, 78). It was located east of Salinas.

If he had wished, Bachelot would have been welcomed by the order of the Sacred Hearts Fathers in Valparaiso, Chile. They could always use another missionary hand. Presumably he stationed himself at the San Gabriel Mission and carried the Gospels from that area. He preferred, he said, to stay in touch with the Sandwich Islands Mission. He had the hope that it would again spring to life. Indeed, that would come to pass.

CHAPTER EIGHT

The Screws are Turned

Meanwhile, on Oʻahu the persecutions had not stopped. If anything they may have been stepped up. The small colony of native Catholic converts was still forced to continue work on the stone walls of the Waikīkī plain despite the forced departure of the two priests.

One prisoner, Agatha Kamoohula, found it necessary to leave her task to relieve herself. A guard then beat her so cruelly with a stick that it broke over her back. Agatha suffered acute pain.

Fortunately, a Protestant church member saw what had happened and scolded the guard for his cruelty. This gentleman's interference was effective, for thereafter the guards gave more liberty to the Catholic prisoners.

In March of 1832, Kaʻahumanu visited the group to encourage them to attend the Protestant services. She particularly solicited the help of Esther, knowing of her influence upon her co-workers. But the effort was unsuccessful for Esther refused to help the queen turn the women into Protestants.

Three months later, on June 5, 1832, the ailing queen dowager was dead, following a lingering illness. It is believed that she was sixty-four years old. She was indeed one of the history-makers of Hawaiʻi. When he learned of Kaʻahumanu's death, the Prefect Apostolic of the Pacific region, Father Bachelot, was more charitable than many might expect. He depicted her as a victim of ill-informed advisors. He wrote in his journal:

> Kaahumanu supports the Calvinists with all her power; she is a woman of much character, a friend of the general good and of order. As the Protestant missionaries have been the first ones to inveigh against the existing disorders, she is prejudiced in their favor; the unlimited docility she shows for them comes from the confidence they have succeeded in inspiring her with. She is under an illusion, but she means well. She has persecuted us because she has been unable to distinguish between truth and error. This much we can credit her for, even when taking into account the unfavorable reports some think to revile her with.
>
> (Yzendoorn, 79–80)

Yzendoorn expresses the opinion that Ka'ahumanu "was one of the most resolute adversaries of the Catholic Religion in Hawaii, and never swayed for a moment from the course of persecution she had determined upon. However, even the victims of her ill-inspired zeal recognized the purity of her intentions" (79).

By the next month the successor to Ka'ahumanu had been named by the chiefs. It was not Kauikeaouli, for the king (Kamehameha III) was still a minor, too young to wield the theoretical scepter or sit on the theoretical throne. It would be Princess Kīna'u, then twenty-seven years old. She was the daughter of King Kamehameha the Great and the wife of Kekūanaō'a, governor of O'ahu and a high chief. She, a *kuhina nui* (premier), would carry on where Ka'ahumanu left off. "She continued the policy of strictly enforcing laws inspired by missionary teachings. In this way she often collided with the young and willful king" (Day *Biographical*, 78). But a couple years later this was to change, writes Day, when the young king became "reconciled with Kinau and agreed to proclaim a code that would punish evil doers."

If the persecuted Catholics hoped for a more lenient persecutor, or a friend on the throne, they were much mistaken. Father Bachelot called Kīna'u "Our greatest enemy" (80), and with cause. In a public address Kīna'u announced her intentions to carry out her predecessor's wishes, and an occasion soon presented itself.

The same month that Kīna'u took over the reins of government the workers on the Waikīkī walls had completed their work and prepared to go home. But, for their refusal to bend to the Protestant rule, they were told by the guards they would each have to build five more fathoms—or thirty feet—of walls. Also, some women would be made to work with "lewd women" and would be employed in cutting bog-rush and in building mud dikes in the swamps.

One observer, historian J. N. Reynolds, writes: "One woman was seen with an infant on her back, bearing large stones in her arms for building this wall! And this punishment was inflicted because they were Catholics, and would not change their religion for that of the missionaries of the Island..." (Reynolds, 417, in Yzendoorn, 82).

The British consul, Richard Charlton, at one point persuaded the king and the chiefs to release all prisoners who were being punished for the sake of religion. The persecutions ceased, but, writes Yzendoorn, "only for the moment" (83).

The lull in the persecutions came to an end shortly after the arrival of the Seventh Company of Protestant missionaries from New England on June 6, 1835. The event, followed by the annual meeting of all the missionaries, seems to have caused a renewed religious activity and persecution of the "followers of the Pope."

The two women, Kilika and Lahina, were set to work gathering excrement from the prison and roadside in this period. They endured the jeers of bystanders gathered in the lane as the women carried this refuse to dump in the ocean. Their freedom finally came six months later when they were released so that they might make mats for the chiefs.

If by this type of punishment the government expected to persuade other natives to follow the Bingham trail, they were mistaken, for a number of natives admired the constancy and faith of the persecuted and asked to be instructed in the faith of these neophytes. So indignant were the foreigners at this religious persecution that both the British and American consuls (Charlton and Jones) remonstrated with Kīna'u that the prisoners be released. It might have happened, says Yzendoorn, had not Bingham, on August 8, sided with Kīna'u saying "that all Hawaiians ought to be of one mind" (89).

In retrospect it is hard to understand how during the persecutions the Reverend Bingham neither "saw and heard chains, whips or instruments of torture" (90). All of these were inflicted upon various Catholic prisoners, and within sight of Kīna'u's residence, where Bingham frequently called. Yzendoorn observes that "far from recommending milder forms of 'conversion' Bingham repeatedly preached against the Papists with such vehemence that the American residents who heard him were greatly incensed" (90). One of these was the American consul, John C. Jones, who in 1840 expressed his concerns at great length in a special *Suppliment* [sic] of the *Sandwich Island Mirror*.

A year later, in 1841, a representation of the Protestant Mission called on the chiefs, questioning them as to the manner in which punishment was meted out to the Catholics. The committee consisted of Messrs. Chamberlain, Armstrong and Castle. One of their concerns was the treatment rendered to Simeon (Kimeone).

> Kimeone Paele...was beaten in the most cruel manner,
> kicked, trampled upon and spit upon by members of the
> Protestant church, but more *feelingly* so by a Mr. John Ii, a
> native, *celebrated for his piety,* who sought every opportunity
> and devised every means in his power to augment the
> torture and suffering of this miserable man.
>
> (*Suppliment*, 23, in Yzendoorn, 90)

Since many of the punishments were carried out in public,
it was only natural that news of this nature captured public
interest. The October 28, 1841, issue of *The Polynesian* carried a
series of questions and answers regarding the punishments
meted out to the "Romanists." The identity of the interrogators
is not given. Among the questions and the replies, perhaps the
one most typical is the following:

> Q. What was the punishment for their crimes?
>   A. It was confinement in prison; if not this, cutting stone
> [from the coral reefs], or if not this, then building stone
> fences; and if anyone continued to make difficulty—
> worshiping idols—five times, then he was sentenced to
> gather up the filth of the Fort and carry it off.
>
> (Yzendoorn, 90)

The lengthy responses to the interrogators were signed by
seven chiefs, including Kekūanaō'a and John I'i. The latter, a
close friend of Bingham, was a member of the Royal House of
Nobles and in 1846 became an associate member of the Supreme
Court.

Persecutions on the other islands occurred over the same
period of time but were much less severe than on O'ahu where
the Catholic natives were forever under governmental and
Protestant eyes. In fact, to escape those persecutions many

natives fled to Moloka'i, the closest island. Father Robert Schoofs states, "On the other islands the Catholics were deprived 'of their lands and [by] declaring ocean and mountains kapu meant that the culprits could neither fish nor fetch wood [for fuel]'" (Schoofs, 25). Nor did the persecutions cease with the royal grant of religious liberty. Under one form or another, Catholics continued to be harassed until about 1850.

On Hawai'i Island, the young chief Lele'iohoku, the son of high chief Kalanimoku, was the only friend in high places that the Catholics had. For his mixing with Catholics and sometimes joining them in prayer he was severely reprimanded. "Shortly afterwards Leleiohoku was ostracized and most of his lands confiscated" (Schoofs, 124).

CHAPTER NINE

The Return of the Exiled

Brother Melchior, who had escaped the exile meted out to the two priests, was not ordained and thus unable to say Mass for the natives who wished it. This allowed him to remain behind and he was able to visit and console the native prisoners, often taking them food. His words of comfort were welcomed by the neophytes left behind by Fathers Bachelot and Short.

He would eventually get some relief. First came another lay brother, Columba Murphy, also a member of the French order of the Sacred Hearts. Columba was not assigned to Honolulu by his religious order. He was there only on a visit. He had departed Bordeaux in 1833 and arrived in the Society Islands the following year, then proceeded to Honolulu. He was safe from persecution because he was a British subject, and not an ordained priest of the Catholic Church. Another helper was part of a French missionary movement that came from Paris to the colonies below the equator, an ordained priest named Desire (Louis) Maigret. (He would later become Bishop of the Sandwich Islands Vicariate.)

Brother Columba stayed only long enough to give Melchior an extra hand and also to form some impressions. When Kīnaʻu learned of his presence, she summoned him to her residence.

She queried him about his purpose and why he had not presented himself to her upon arrival. She was less than pleased with his presence, and suspicious of his motives. Not so the young king, who treated him with courtesy.

During his short visit, Columba gathered some impressions as to the state of the Catholic faith in Honolulu. One was that the situation was favorable enough for the return of the two exiled clergymen. He went to Monterey County in California hoping to find Father Short, but he was away. It was Columba's intention to inform Short and Bachelot (at San Gabriel) that it was probably safe to return to Honolulu. It turned out to be bad advice, but it was heeded.

Father Bachelot, cheered by Columba's observation, remained on the lookout for an opportunity to return to his mission in the Sandwich Islands. That came March 28, 1837 when the brig *La Clementine* sailed from Santa Barbara, California, for Honolulu. The reluctant Captain Handley agreed to their passage when offered five hundred dollars. The vessel was owned by the Honolulu Frenchman and consul, Jules Dudoit. But it sailed under British colors. Twenty days later, April 17, it dropped anchor at Honolulu.

As soon as it tied up to the wharf trouble began. The priests were recognized, despite Short having grown a long beard. Governor Kekūanaōʻa was at the landing and soon learned that Father Bachelot was also on board, but initially too ill to debark. It was the beginning of a long and tedious process by which the government again tried to expel them both as soon as possible. It was déja vu.

Eventually Kekūanaōʻa ordered the two priests to re-embark immediately and at once. Bachelot pleaded that he would only stay a short time, that he wished to go on to Ponape to help form a Catholic mission in Micronesia. His request was granted with the admonition to be gone soon. And Short was told to depart on *La Clementine*, but the captain refused to take him.

Governor Kekūanaōʻa put his frustrations in writing on April 19, 1837. The English translation, which accompanied it, ran as follows:

> This is what I have to say to the French gentleman [sic]. This is my opinion to both of you who were sent away before from these Islands, that you are forever forbidden by our chiefs to come here, this is the reason. I asked you if you intended to live here, the answer you made was—no, we intend to stop for a few days until we can obtain a vessel to carry us from here. I replied When you get a vessel, go quickly. This is what I say to both of you: Now this time prepare you to depart in the same vessel in which you arrived: when the vessel is ready both of you are to go without delay.
>
> Na Kekuanaoa.
>
> Printed at the Oahu Printing Establishment.
>
> (Yzendoorn, 100)

The Oahu Printing Establishment was the missionary press.

Back and forth went the priests, the government and the United States and British consuls, as well as the defiant Captain Handley and the sympathetic ship owner, Jules Dudoit. The two lay brothers at the Catholic mission were forbidden to offer shelter to the two priests. Dispatches in the form of short letters flew among Kekuanaoa and the consuls, the ship owner, the priests and Kīnaʻu who was determined to rid herself of these meddlesome priests. Protests on the part of the consuls and the priests were to no avail. When the two priests were escorted by the police to *La Clementine*, its mate ordered the tender off, telling the native officers that no persons would be forced aboard while he was in charge. The small party returned to the wharf, then back to the ship again where this time they were indeed forced aboard.

More orders. More stalling. Even the young king was involved. From his Lahaina residence he sent a letter to Kīna'u ordering and authorizing her to place these two men on a vessel that would take them away, emphasizing that an additional religion had no place in Hawai'i. Yzendoorn called it the beginning of a "kind of epistolary war, the din of which sounded unto the utmost boundaries of the Pacific" (104).

Even the commanders of the English and French men-of-war ships were involved. "The exchange of communication (accusatory) was voluminous, and Jones contributed far more than his share" (Gast, 148).

It was nearing the end of May. *La Clementine* had been in the harbor with its two refugees since April 1837. But the battle was far from over. British officers were involved, inasmuch as rights of a British subject (Short) were of concern. It was a situation far more complicated than the original banishment. Heels of both parties were firmly dug in. Vessel upon vessel refused passage to the priests, until finally Father Short was given passage on the ship *Peru* on October 30, 1837. It had been an eight-month dispute. Father Short, after a brief stay in Tahiti, arrived at Valparaiso the following January, the headquarters for the Sacred Hearts Fathers in the New World.

A fresh annoyance was to present itself only a few days after the departure of Father Short. The schooner *Europa* sailed into Honolulu harbor and among its passengers were two other Catholic priests. One of them was Father Maigret. The other was Father Columba Murphy, the lay brother who had for a short time visited Honolulu before going to Valparaiso. He was now no longer a lay brother but an ordained Catholic priest, anathema to the rulers of Hawai'i. Governor Kekuanaoa, husband of premier Kīna'u, came aboard and asked for a certified statement that the "missionaries would not preach Papal doctrines, nor officiate according to Catholic rites, and that they did not know the teachings of the Pope" (Yzendoorn, 114–15).

Since no ordained Catholic priest would conscientiously sign such a statement they responded obliquely:

The undersigned passengers on board the *Europa* promise not to interfere with the laws and regulations of the Sandwich Islands during their sojourn, and to leave the islands at the first favorable opportunity.

J.C. Murphy

L. Maigret

(Bingham *Residence*, 512, in Yzendoorn, 115)

This was far from what the Hawaiian government (or the missionaries) would accept, and in short order Kīna'u (who preferred to call herself Ka'ahumanu II) fired off a response demanding specifics.

Salutations to you L. Maigret and J.C. Murphy aboard the ship *Europa*. I have received your writing today and have seen what you have made known, but you have not stated definitely to me in writing what countrymen you are and what your employments and how long you wish to stay. You have not informed me in your writing to what country you wish to go by the first available opportunity.

On this account I request you to make a clear statement of these points in writing, and if you are priests of the religion of the pope or of any other office, make it known to me, do not hide it from me, for this is the only reason why I hesitate to allow you to land. I do not desire propagators of that religion to dwell here, that is tabu.

By me Kaahumanu II.

Honolulu, Nov. 2, 1837.

(ibid.)

The following morning Dudoit carried to the premier herself the reply of Maigret.

This certifies that I, Louis Maigret, a Frenchman, came on board the ship *Europa* at Valparaiso, and my object was to remain here until I could get a passage to the Marquesas or the Dangerous Archipelago Islands, and that I will conform to the laws and regulations of Government at all times.

L. Maigret.

(ibid.)

It was an evasive response. Nor did Father Murphy make any reply inasmuch as he did not want to disclose his ordination and lose the chance of landing. The declaration of the British consul that Murphy was not a priest was less than the truth, but on that basis Murphy was allowed to land.

Kīna'u pinned Dudoit down. Was the writer of the letter a Catholic priest? The French agent said he was. In vain Dudoit pleaded the case of his countryman, Maigret. When this failed, he told Kīna'u he would renew his request in writing, and asked for her reply in writing so that he might send these documents to the French government.

A few days later, Kīna'u addressed Dudoit in a lengthy letter, setting forth the position of the king and the kingdom. It said in part:

We protect all strangers, but on account of former difficulties and dissensions, our minds are made up not to consent that Roman Catholic priests come here, from any country....I make known to you respecting the Romish priest Maigret. He concealed from me his country, and his being a priest, as he wished to land privately and dwell, and we could not remove him....I cannot confide in his word. If the Governments of France and England and America desire the peace and quiet of my country and my king, they will allow us to enforce our laws prohibiting

the priests of the Roman Catholic religion. ...moreover let
M.Maigret go away in the ship in which he came and you
will please make known my letter to the Government of
France with kindness.

By authority of the King,

Kaahumanu II.

Honolulu, Nov. 8, 1837.

(Wyllie, 293, in Yzendoorn, 116)

Maigret's brief letter of reply denied he had concealed that
he was a priest and his home country. It made no impression.
With Father Short off to New World mission headquarters in
Valparaiso, Bachelot realized his mission in Honolulu would
not be fulfilled. He would venture to Micronesia. But the vessel
that Bachelot was awaiting to carry him to Ponape failed to
arrive. An ill but determined Bachelot arranged to purchase the
schooner *Honolulu* from Jules Dudoit. He agreed to pay three
thousand dollars for it, in two installments. It was rechristened
Nôtre Dame de Paix (Our Lady of Peace) and it left Honolulu for
Ponape (the modern Pohnpei) November 23, 1837, with Fathers
Maigret and Bachelot aboard.

CHAPTER TEN

Death Comes
to the Pioneer Prelate

Father Bachelot had not fared well at San Gabriel. Plagued by intermittent illness, he nevertheless seemed to recover and was in good health and good spirits en route to Hawai'i aboard the *La Clementine*. It was, perhaps, his finest moment in a time that had dealt him controversy and abuse—but it was not to last. When in December 1837 he boarded the *Nôtre Dame de Paix* bound for Ponape, his health began to deteriorate, and the end came swiftly.

According to Father Maigret, Father Bachelot's mind began to wander as his body began to shut down. In a delirium he talked constantly, and longingly spoke of a hope that before he died he would see the Bishop of Nilopolis (Brazil).

It was not to be.

After two weeks at sea, Father Maigret knew the end was coming. He gave his fellow priest the Sacrament of Anointing the Sick, the final rites of the Catholic Church. Early on the morning of December 5, 1837, Bachelot breathed his last. Eight days later, the ship stood off Ponape, the place Father Bachelot felt called to serve, but was never to see. On December 14, he was buried on the shore of a small Micronesian island called Na (Napali), near the mouth of the Metalanim harbor. He had come to Ponape at last, and he would never leave it.

Father Maigret would not forget his friend. In February 1838, he enlisted the help of natives to build a small but suitable mausoleum–chapel to hold the remains of the departed pioneer priest. Yzendoorn notes that despite Father Maigret's good intentions, "the last resting place of the first Catholic priest who preached the gospel in the Northern Pacific, the exact place can no longer be found" (Yzendoorn, 120).

It was not the final effort to mark the site, for twenty-one years later another missionary planted a tree in recognition of Father Bachelot's devotion. But this time it was a Hawai'i-born Protestant, the Reverend Dr. Luther Gulick, who planted a coconut "on the grave of the man, who, though under a separate banner, had struggled for the honor of the same Master" (ibid.). Again, however, it was nature that had the last word. In 1905 yet another hurricane savaged Ponape and trees were uprooted.

Today, somewhere on those distant islands, lie the remains of a man whose life was spent in the service of God and his fellow man. The remains are hidden, probably forever, but the memory of this good man of God is still vibrant, held in great esteem.

In the February 1860 issue of *The Friend*, the Reverend Dr. Gulick paid quiet homage to Father Bachelot.

> A few weeks since I planted a foreign cocoanut tree on the grave of the Rev. Mr. Bachelot...on his way from the Sandwich Islands to Ascension [Pohnpei]. ...He was buried in a dense cocoanut grove on the island of Na. ...Though differing widely from him in religious faith, and condemning much of his missionary life, I respect his zeal, and most especially desire to honor his devotion to the enterprise of spreading Christianity. Had his successors

followed up his work in Micronesia rather than the Sandwich Islands, this field would have undoubtedly been their own, in all its extent. (120)

In Honolulu today a street carries his name, and in the Makiki district a prominent church facility bears the Bachelot name. He would be pleased, after all these years, to find his works and deeds still remembered.

CHAPTER ELEVEN

The Law of the Land

Great was the ire and frustration of premier Kīna'u and the young king, Kamehameha III, when the two banished priests returned in 1837. To worsen matters they brought with them another papist, Father Louis Maigret. Drastic steps must be taken, they decided, not only to rid the country of these trouble-making priests but also to curb Catholic persuasion throughout the nation.

The "throne" saw that its weakness lay in having no laws to enforce its wishes and demands. To correct the situation, they enlisted the Protestant clergyman William Richards, one of the missionaries who "had severed his connections with the ABCFM and entered the services of the government as translator and political advisor" (Yzendoorn, 128). In the latter capacity his hand is detected in many of the communications that emanated from the throne. He would serve his community well.

It was with Richards' guidance that a law was drawn up, its aim to prevent any future priestly difficulties. So much for those earlier ABCFM instructions to the missionaries that "you are to abstain from all interference with local and political interests of the people" (HMCS, 17). The following document was issued from the Protestant press at the Lahainaluna Seminary.

AN ORDINANCE
Rejecting the Catholic Religion

As we have seen the peculiarities of the Catholic religion and the proceedings of the priests of the Roman faith to be calculated to set man against man in our kingdom, and as we formerly saw that disturbance was made in the time of Kaahumanu I, and as it was on this account that the priests of the Roman faith were banished and sent away from this kingdom, and as from that time they have been under sentence of banishment until within this past year when we have been brought into new and increased trouble on account of those who follow the Pope; and as our determination to keep away such persons is by no means recent, and also on the request of foreigners that we make it known in writing. Therefore, I, with my chiefs, forbid, by this document that anyone should teach the peculiarities of the Pope's religion, nor shall it be allowed to any one who teaches those doctrines or peculiarities to reside in this kingdom; nor shall the ceremonies be exhibited in our kingdom, nor shall any one teaching its peculiarities or its faith be permitted to land on these shores; for it is not proper that two religions be found in this small kingdom. Therefore we utterly refuse to allow anyone to teach these peculiarities in any manner whatsoever. We moreover prohibit all vessels whatsoever from bringing any teacher of that religion into this kingdom.

Any vessel that shall bring in a teacher of the Pope's religion or of anything similar, and wishes to enter the harbor on business may enter, subject however to these regulations, viz. no teacher on board his ship shall by any means be permitted to come ashore, because all such have been strictly prohibited from this Kingdom. If any such teacher should come ashore, he shall be seized and returned to the vessel which he left. And the vessel in which he came shall not leave, except he shall sail with it.

And if any shall come on shore without liberty and shall be concealed until the vessel in which he came shall have sailed and afterwards shall be discovered, he shall remain a prisoner until a proper vessel can be obtained for him to return and then he shall go after having paid to the chiefs a fine at their discretion.

But if it should be impossible for the said person to dwell on board, it shall be permitted him in writing to dwell for a season on shore, on his having given bonds and security for the protection of the kingdom.

If the master of the vessel shall refuse to obey this law and shall set on shore the teacher prohibited by this act, in contempt of the government, then the vessel shall be forfeited to the chiefs of these islands and become theirs, and the cargo on board the vessel shall likewise become theirs, and the master shall pay the sum of ten thousand dollars, but it may be optional with the chiefs to remit any part of the sum.

Moreover if the stranger should present himself as a mechanic, a merchant or of any other business, and it shall be granted him to reside here, and afterwards he shall be found teaching the doctrine of the Pope or any thing else whereby this kingdom shall be disturbed, this law shall be in force against him and he may be retained a prisoner or banished, after he shall have paid a fine at the discretion of the chiefs.

That this law may be extensively known, it shall be printed and published, and on the arrival of a vessel, it shall be the duty of the Pilot to carry with him this law and give it to the master of the vessel that he may not be ignorant of the law. And if the law is not shown to the master of the vessel by the Pilot and any prohibited person come ashore because the Pilot did not show this law to the master of the vessel, the Pilot shall pay to the chiefs one hundred dollars; and the person who left the vessel shall be returned on board again.

If any one, either foreigner or native, shall be found assisting another in teaching the doctrine of the Pope's religion, he shall pay to the government a fine of one hundred dollars for each offense.

KAMEHAMEHA III.
Lahaina, Maui
December 18, 1837
(Yzendoorn, 121–22)

✠ ✠ ✠

Yzendoorn observed that by this ordinance Congregationalism "was incidentally made the religion of the State, and to natives and foreigners no choice was left but between that particular brand of Protestantism and some broad Deism" (122).

To escape the enforcement of these rigid restrictions, as a matter of conscience, a group of native Catholics left Honolulu for the distant district of Wai'anae. There they were protected by a friendly chief. Their religious freedom would be curtailed several months later when Chiefess Kekāuluohi had them captured and forced to march back to the city.

Now, with the priests banished again, their opponents felt the full flush of victory. Revival was in the air. Why stop at just a law that would put Catholicism in its place? Other moral matters soon came into focus. Baptisms by the thousands were gained thanks to the effectiveness of the eminent preacher and scholar, the Hilo-based Reverend Titus Coan. Kuykendall writes of him as "...a man of broad culture and human sympathy, a preacher of great power, like one of the old Hebrew prophets, the evangelist par excellence" (115).

This religious excitement led the ministers to look into the matter of grogshops. There were too many and too much dispensed in the way of spirits. In March 1838, all but two of the Honolulu grogshops were closed down. A week later no one could sell spirits of any kind without a proper license. A fine of ten dollars was assessed on any saloon keeper at whose place of business a man was intoxicated. The fine was increased by ten dollars for every repetition. When it was seen that these liquor laws were not sufficient, "a more stringent one was promulgated August 21, 1838, absolutely prohibiting the importation of all distilled spirits" (123).

Yzendoorn noted that the "missionaries also opposed strongly, but perhaps less judiciously, the use of tobacco and coffee. The smoker of tobacco was excommunicated from church membership, and stranger yet, he was written up, together with the drinker of spirits, to the place which is the habitat of burning spirits, and from whence everlasting smoke ascends" (ibid.).

Kīna'u, the premier who styled herself Ka'ahumanu II, died in 1839, after a short illness, at the age of thirty-two. She had given the Catholics a hard time during her rulership of seven years. Father Bachelot had called her "our worst enemy." But author Yzendoorn was more forgiving: "We may still attribute her persecution to religious zeal, which, however misguided, may have gotten its reward from a merciful God, whose justice takes into account the circumstances which lessen and excuse from sin, as well as those that aggravate it" (127).

Nor was the fire of persecution dampened in this period of great zeal for Hawai'i's salvation. Six more Catholic natives were to feel the sting of being "followers of the Pope." These neophytes were Lui Keliiolono, Paulo Kelili, Ana Kuili, Hilario Kapo, Kalala Oupai and Malaaho. Taken to the fort three days later they appeared before Governor Kekuanaoa for "examination." Like other Catholic converts, they were to be punished not because of their religion, but because "they had disobeyed the laws of the land which forbade idolatry" (125). By this time that was a well-worn, tired and false argument.

A few days later a contributor to the *Sandwich Island Gazette* found that five "Catholic convicts were forced into the manufacture of mud bricks" (*Gazette*, 7 July 1839, in Yzendoorn, 125).

Yzendoorn noted that the governor, who was "judge, jury and a Presbyterian," informed the prisoners that Popery and idolatry were identical (125).

Three months later Kīna'u's successor was named premier, again a female. Her Christian name was Miriam but she is generally known as Chiefess Kekāuluohi. The new *kuhina nui* was "a stern chiefess" (Day *Biographical*, 74). The Reverend Bingham says that this good lady "entered into her public duties with much propriety" (Bingham *Residence*, 534, in Yzendoorn, 127). Yzendoorn reported that this propriety "consisted in the arrest of no less than sixty-seven Catholics, men, women and children, who by her order were brought to Honolulu from Waianae, over thirty miles distant, where for some time they had taken refuge" (127–128). She had sought them out, pursued them to their place of refuge and, under guard, forced them to travel on foot from the Wai'anae coast to Honolulu.

When the group was less than three miles from Honolulu, one John Kaluahiva, only thirty-seven years old, fatigued and worn out, lay by the roadside to rest. Left there, without friends or family, he expired that night, near the village of Maunalua, site of the present-day Fort Shafter.

The next day the prisoners were interrogated by the chiefs, where they pleaded guilty to the crime of "popery." A spokesman for the missionaries would have them know they were not being punished for their religion but for disobeying the laws of the kingdom, for idolatry, a distinction without a difference.

After the chiefs' interrogation, all but thirteen were dismissed. These unfortunates were taken for confinement to the fort. The *Sandwich Island Gazette* reported,

The hand of one person was lashed to that of another, and arms raised over a partition seven feet high, which passed between each couple, who also had their feet in chains. On Sunday morning, exhausted by fatigue and pain, nine were liberated and the succeeding day the remaining four, two men and two women, all promised to obey the laws.

(*Sandwich Island Gazette*, June 22, 1839, in Yzendoorn, 128)

Perhaps two of the most ignominious persecutions were those inflicted upon two Hawaiian women. Juliana Kanakanui was about fifty. The other, Maria Makalena Kaha, was twenty years younger. Charged with being Catholics, they were taken to the fort where they were interrogated. Repeatedly ordered to abandon the Catholic religion and embrace the faith of Bingham, they steadfastly refused.

Juliana was then "brought up to a withered hau tree, her hands placed on each side of one of its dead branches, about seven-feet high and then shackled with irons so that she might be said to hang by the wrists, as she could barely touch the ground with her toes.

The other woman was brought to the eaves of a low thatched house, where her arms were forced around one of the rafters, about six feet in height and then made fast by irons, and she stood with her face so near the thatch that it was constantly lacerated by the stubs of grass which she was unable to avoid. During the night heavy showers poured down upon the helpless women.

(Yzendoorn, 131)

The same source tells us that the next morning a number of foreigners gathered to witness the scene of persecution. The governor, absent at the time, knew of the arrest of the two women, whom he intended to "examine" the following morning. The two victims, having been in "that awful position for eighteen hours, without drink or food of any description were in a most pitiful state" (ibid.).

Jules Dudoit, the Frenchman, and another unnamed gentleman, gave some money to relatives of the women, instructing them to buy the sufferers some poi and fish. About this time, one of the Protestant missionaries, the Reverend Artemus Bishop, made his appearance and it was then that the guards began releasing the women's bonds. But they did so with abusive language. It is to the credit of the foreigners and the Reverend Bishop that the women were released.

A Father Arsenius (Robert) Walsh had made his appearance sometime after the banishment of the two priests. His arrival from Valparaiso was well after the death of Ka'ahumanu. It was thought by his superiors in Valparaiso that this young priest, "being a British subject, would have a greater chance of success than a French priest. After a brief hesitation on the part of the rulers, he was ordered to depart, but the timely arrival of the French ship of war *La Bonite* created a diversion in his favor..." (Kuykendall, 144).

Walsh was barely tolerated by the regime. For his permission to remain he could thank Captain Russell Elliot of Her British Majesty's ship *Fly*. Having arrived from Valparaiso, Elliot "exerted himself in behalf of liberty of conscience, and besought the premier to restore freedom to the prisoners who for religion's sake were then in bondage" (*Suppliment*, 55, in Yzendoorn, 125). Yzendoorn observed that more forcible arguments were needed to cure the Hawaiian leaders of their ill-advised mania for persecution.

The persecutions did not cease for nine prisoners sentenced to hard labor in 1836, 1837 and 1838. They were confined in two little huts at the edge of the city "where they were closely watched by an officer of the government." Father Walsh insisted that the Protestant ministers liberate these nine individuals. His request went unheeded. Similarly, requests for Catholic burial services were also curtly denied. The expected "niceties" of cooperation among Christian sects were not honored.

The Spanish-born Don Francisco de Paula Marin, the man who had rendered so many eminent services to the islands, while on his deathbed, was denied the consolation of receiving the sacrament of the dying from a priest. At his grave site the services were "performed by a minister of a sect he had repudiated" (126).

In early 1839, Camillo Especiano, a Mexican gentleman, had died suddenly and "an application was made to the governor to allow Father Walsh to perform the ceremonies of the Catholic Church over the remains of this man who had been raised a Catholic. The request was curtly denied" (ibid.). In a communication to Kīna'u, the English commander was quite specific in regards to the Catholic problem. In very emphatic terms he informed her "that Catholics are not idolaters, and that those who informed her that they were had done so either in ignorance or in malice, and that the less she had to do with such advisors, the better for herself and her people" (125).

Little did Father Walsh and the prisoners know that the persecutions were about to end, almost literally with a bang. On July 9, 1839, a ship was rounding Diamond Head. A signal was heard from its booming cannon. The French frigate *L'Artemise* was soon riding the blue waters of Honolulu harbor. It would announce the "dawn of religious freedom for the Sandwich Islanders" (133) .

CHAPTER 12

Gunboat Diplomacy

On June 16, 1839, a month before the French frigate *L'Artemise* showed up off Honolulu, an American whaler, the *Elizabeth*, anchored at the harbor. It had sailed from Tahiti a month earlier. It brought to the Protestant missionaries letters from their South Seas brethren, along with news that a French warship, *L'Artemise*, bound for Honolulu, had struck an uncharted reef off Point Venus in Tahiti. The mishap would delay its arrival at the Sandwich Islands. This news alerted the powers that be that they might well clean up their act and be on their best behavior, for there could be repercussions for the past treatment of the French priests.

The editor of the *Sandwich Island Gazette* surmised as much.

What may be the object of the Artemise to this island is not known; it is possible the Commander may be clothed with power to demand justice for wrongs and insults that have been offered by this people to the subjects and the Flag of France. The day of account, we are certain, cannot be far distant, and when it does come, we hope that the whole truth will be manifest; and that those who have been instrumental in leading these credulous people into trouble and difficulty, will have to bear the burden of helping them out. We do say, and we believe it to be the truth, that the Chiefs and Rulers of this land would never have committed the outrages they have, had they not been led on by indiscreet advisors, and biased by the ipse dixit of meddling busy bodies, who, with false notions of justice and power, have used their ill-merited influence to draw the lords of these Isles into controversy with one of the most powerful nations of the globe. We entertain no animosity or ill-will toward those who are in power in this land where we sojourn, they have our best wishes for their prosperity and advancement, but we do hope that the King of the French will teach them a lesson, never to be forgotten; that they may remember in future that in their intercourse with the people of foreign nations, injustice, inhumanity, and oppression will not for a moment be tolerated for any cause whatever which may be assigned.

(*Sandwich Island Gazette*, June 22, 1839, in Yzendoorn, 130)

When Captain Laplace dropped anchor in Honolulu harbor on July 9, 1839, he came not as a trader, ready to buy and barter. Nor was his a friendly mission, or merely a vessel en route to some other Pacific archipelago. A few months earlier, while in Sydney, Australia, Laplace received orders from his king, Louis Philippe, to proceed to Honolulu and there lay down rigid terms regarding the treatment of French subjects, and Catholics in particular. Matters of fair trade would be secondary. The terms which Laplace laid out were designated a Manifesto. It was not a document drawn up hastily. Doubtless it had been carefully prepared after he left Sydney, or in Tahiti at the latest. Much thought had been given to its composition. Laplace made a series of clear demands and laid out in detail the terms to be met.

According to Laplace himself, the native authorities so well understood the reasons of his coming [probably thanks to the advance news from the Elizabeth] that even before the vessel had established any communication with the shore all the Catholics who were then still employed in the performance of public works, held prisoners for conscience's sake, were to be immediately set at liberty, although many were liberated only three days later.

(Laplace, 439, in Yendoorn, 134)

Aware of the possibility that some foreign intervener, such as the British, might appear on the scene and jeopardize the French mission, Laplace lost no time in making known the purpose of the vessel's presence. Within three hours of his arrival, one of his officers was dispatched to deliver the lengthy document to the ruling chiefs. It read:

MANIFESTO addressed to the King of the Sandwich Islands by the naval Captain Laplace, Commander of the French frigate l'Artemise in the name of his government.

His Majesty the King of the French having commanded me to come to Honolulu in order to put an end either by force or by persuasion to the ill-treatment of which the French are the victims at the Sandwich Islands.

I hasten first to employ the latter means as being more in harmony with their noble and liberal political system pursued by France toward weaker nations, hoping that I shall thus make the king and the principle chiefs of these islands understand how fatal to their interests the conduct is which they pursue towards her, and which may cause disasters to themselves and their country should they persist in it.

Misled by perfidious counsels, deceived by the excessive indulgence of which my country has given evidence in their favor for several years, they doubtless do not know how powerful France is, and that there is no power in the world which is capable of preventing it from punishing its enemies; otherwise they would have endeavored to merit its good will, instead of displeasing it as they have done by ill treating the French; they would have faithfully kept the treaties instead of violating them, as soon as the fear whereby bad intentions have constrained, had disappeared with the man-of-war which had caused it; in fine they would have understood that persecuting the Catholic religion, tarnishing it with the name of idolatry, and expelling under this absurd pretext, the French from this archipelago, was to offer an insult to France and its sovereign.

It is without doubt the formal intention of France, that the king of the Sandwich Islands be powerful, independent of every foreign power, and that he consider her his ally; but she also demands that he conforms to usages established by civilized nations. Now among the latter there is not one that does not permit in its territory the free exercise of all religions; and, however, in the Sandwich Islands the Catholics are not allowed to exercise theirs publicly, whilst the Methodists [sic] enjoy there the most extended privileges; for the latter all favors, for the former nothing but the most cruel persecutions. Such a state of affairs being contrary to international law, insulting to Catholic nations, cannot last any longer, and I am sent to put an end to it. Consequently, I demand in the name of my Sovereign:

1. That the Catholic worship be declared free throughout the islands which are subject to the king of the Sandwich Islands. The members of this communion shall enjoy all the privileges granted to Protestants.

2. That the site for a Catholic church be granted by the government at Honolulu, a port frequented by the

French and that this church be ministered by priests of their nationality.

3. That all Catholics imprisoned on account of religion since the last persecutions inflicted upon the Catholic missionaries be at once set at liberty.

4. That the king of the Sandwich Islands deposit in the hands of the captain of l'Artemise the sum of twenty thousand dollars as a guarantee of his future conduct towards France, which sum will be restored to him by the government of that country as soon as it shall judge that the clauses of the accompanying treaty shall have been faithfully executed.

5. That the treaty signed by the king of the Sandwich Islands, as well as the sum mentioned above, be conveyed on board l'Artemise by one of the principal chiefs of the country, whilst the batteries of Honolulu do salute the French flag with twenty-one guns, which will be returned by the frigate.

But, if contrary to my expectations, it should be otherwise; if the king and principal chiefs of the Sandwich Islands, misled by bad advice, should refuse to sign the treaty which I present, war would immediately commence, and all the devastations, all the calamities which will be the unhappy but inevitable consequences, will be imputed to themselves alone; also they will have to pay the damages, which the foreigners, injured under these circumstances, will have a right to claim.

Honolulu, July the 10th (for the 9th), 1839.

The naval captain commanding the French frigate l'Artemise.

LAPLACE .

(Laplace, 531, in Yzendoorn, 134–5)

It was made clear that ratification of the accompanying treaty would take place before noon July 12. Otherwise hostilities would begin at once. This Laplace made clear when he earlier wrote his own minister in France, "I believe I will be able to bring my negotiations in the Sandwich Islands to a conclusion as successfully as I have in Tahiti...[However] I will not hesitate to employ violence to obtain an exemplary reparation for the insults to France made by the chief of this archipelago, or by those who advise him" (Birkett, 75).

But there was no serious thought of the kingdom resisting these demands, especially from a nation as powerful as France. There was a delay however, due to the young king being at his preferred residence in Lahaina. Until the king could return to Honolulu and participate in the negotiations it was agreed to provide a hostage who would remain aboard the vessel. "The...hostage was John Ii [who] was clearly a puppet of the missionaries. He spoke not a single European language; moreover he was deceitful, puritanical, and critical of everything he observed around him" (ibid.).

The historian Ralph Kuykendall recorded that

The treaty was signed by the kuhina-nui and the governor of Oahu (afterwards ratified by the king), the money, borrowed from local merchants, was taken on board the frigate, and the other stipulations carefully complied with. On the Sunday following, the French commander came on shore with 120 Marines and 60 seamen under arms to attend a military mass which was celebrated by Father Walsh in one of the king's houses.

(Kuykendall, 167)

It must have galled the opponents of the Catholic mission to see this ceremony being conducted right under their collective noses after a decade of its prohibition. Nor were the foreign merchants at all pleased with having to loan the kingdom money to satisfy the French demand for a guarantee. There was grumbling to the effect that "…the money should be taken from the Protestant missionaries" (Yzendoorn, 137).

The demands of the French treaty were effective immediately. The reaction of the entire community, save the Protestant missionaries and their followers, was of joy and jubilation. Wrote Laplace in his journal, "With peace thus established the blockade of the port could be lifted. This enabled a large number of Honolulu's foreign residents to rush out [to the ship] to congratulate me on the peaceful outcome of my negotiations and to thank me for the service I was rendering both themselves and the nation by breaking the bonds in which the Methodists had held them so long" (Birkett, 75).

Even more exuberant, and relieved, was the Hawaiian population, Catholic and non-Catholic alike. They were now free, like everybody else, to practice the religion of their choice. Or none at all, which was the preference of many who had been coerced into attending the Protestant services.

As for the Mass which was celebrated by Father Walsh, Laplace noted that many who filled the crowded building were Protestants who showed their approval of the treaty and came to "express their strong disapproval of the barbarous behavior of the Methodist missionaries toward our fellow Catholics" (ibid.). Laplace was particularly pleased that natives and foreigners alike could experience "a new religious era that had dawned on the Sandwich Islands."

After a more formal, but widely attended, dinner hosted by the French consul, Laplace saw his mission, as ordered by King Louis Philippe, completed, and he returned to his homeland.

Shortly after his return, he was promoted to the rank of a rear-admiral. He had served his king and his nation well, as a diplomat and as a navigator. By the time he died at his home in Brest in 1875, he had served in the French Navy for sixty-five of his eighty-one years. His government had earlier named him one of the nation's ten vice-admirals.

CHAPTER THIRTEEN

A Most Surprising Supporter

In January 1840, the monthly newspaper *The Sandwich Island Mirror* came out with what it called a "Suppliment" [sic]. It was a seventy-two-page article and its main focus was the persecution of native Catholics over the previous ten years. It condemned the severe mistreatment and was specific in identifying many of the victims and the punishment meted out to them. Nor did the article overlook the expulsion of the Catholic priests by Ka'ahumanu, and later on, by Kīna'u.

This lengthy article was published in the *Mirror* only a few months after the Laplace Manifesto, whereby an agreement was reached with the government allowing free practice of religion in the islands. However, the author set out to attack an earlier missionary-related article in the *Hawaiian Spectator,* and document the injustices inflicted upon the Hawaiian Catholics, principally on O'ahu.

The article was not signed, though the editor of the short-lived *Mirror* was R. J. Howard. But the Suppliment itself has long been attributed to John Coffin Jones, the first United States consul to the Kingdom of Hawai'i.

In his opening salvo in the monthly *Mirror,* Jones quarreled with an account in the *Hawaiian Spectator*, the Protestant journal, believed to be from the pen of "Mr. Samuel Castle, a member of the mission family..." (*Suppliment,* 3) Jones asserted that the article was "the joint labor of the whole force of the Mission at Honolulu but palmed upon Mr. Castle because he held only a subordinate position in that body and would therefore be the most convenient person on whom the obloquy of the public should fall in the event that a true statement of facts should perchance come to the world" (ibid.).

Jones uses over 34,000 words to make the case that the Protestant Mission had a heavy hand in the matter of the persecutions over the previous ten years or more. It was the hand behind the throne as it were. Whereas the author, Jones, might have considered it a treatise, others, especially of the Mission, would be more apt to describe it as a diatribe or tirade. Jones is said to have been a complicated, driven and energetic individual, not one to sit back and let his world spin around him. He was a man of means and had a good business background. He was heavily engaged in shipping, at one time owned a couple of vessels, and was generally regarded as an active and successful trader.

He also acted as the Pacific representative of the Boston-based firm of Marshall & Wilde, who were among other matters, heavily engaged in the prosperous sandalwood trade with China. He also had a problem with his marriages. While married to one woman, he later quietly married another. This second wife was Lahilahi Marin, daughter of entrepreneur Don Francisco de Paula Marin. Jones was now tarnished with the label of bigamist.

Particularly annoying to Jones was the Protestant Mission's cozy relationship with the ruling chiefs and sovereigns of the kingdom. He made no secret of his dissatisfaction with the mistreatment of natives who showed any signs of adhering to the Catholic faith, or even having in their homes a rosary or prayer book.

It is especially interesting to learn that Jones was not a Catholic, or a Papist, as the missionaries termed them. Jones was a Unitarian.

At one time he sought to have his American counterparts establish a Unitarian church in Honolulu. When this did not materialize, Jones considered himself a Unitarian minister and acted in that role.

Though not a Catholic, he often attended services in the small Fort Street chapel and remained on good terms with the priests. It is to Jones' credit that he pressed for the complete freedom of religion for all Hawai'i. And, since the Catholics were the prominent target of the government and the Calvinist missionaries, it was in their defense that Jones waged his personal war on behalf of the "Papists." Yet his goal was to "effectively advance the cause of religious freedom by establishing a Unitarian church in Hawaii" (Gast, 73).

Calvinist rigidity was demonstrated when one of the former members of their church who strayed from the faith and fell into intemperance was refused burial services by his former church. Jones rose to the occasion and read the burial service for the person not in good standing with the Protestant Mission. Wrote missionary Levi Chamberlain: "A foreigner was buried this afternoon whose death was hastened by intemperance. Mr. Jones, who is honored by the title of consul, attended and read prayers on the occasion at the grave. The selection would have been appropriate for the burial of a devoted servant of God, one who had died in the Lord for whom we should mourn not as others which have no hope" (Chamberlain, February 22, 1937).

In fact, so much did the missionaries consider Jones a burr under their saddle that they were eventually successful in persuading the Department of State to recall the American Consul from his post. He was replaced by Peter A. Brinsmade. In his defense, which fell upon the deaf Washington ears of Secretary of State Henry Clay, Jones protested that he was within his rights when he complained to the king, Kamehameha III, regarding the matter of religious persecution of Catholics in the kingdom.

Apparently his dismissal from his consulate post was not agreeable to the general population. According to J. N. Reynolds, a lavish testimonial dinner was held in Jones' honor. It was the largest gathering of individuals at one table ever held in Honolulu. The toastmaster, in his laudatory remarks, singled out the honoree as "an advocate of religious and personal freedom" (Gast, 165n).

The expense laid out by the sponsors for the event was said to have been over three thousand dollars. Jones' wordy document made the case that the Protestant Mission had had a heavy hand in the matter of the persecutions.

In his book, *The Contentious Consul*, author Ross Gast makes the statement that "Jones exchanged numerous letters with the king and his advisors and aired his views at great length in the columns of the *Sandwich Island Gazette*." This may be an error, for the *Sandwich Island Mirror* was the vehicle used by Jones, although he undoubtedly expressed himself in other local newspapers, including the *Gazette*.

Jones quite correctly describes the contents of his lengthy writing as "...an account of the persecutions of the Catholics at the Sandwich Islands." In general, the first and fourth quarters of the *Suppliment* deal with demolishing Castle's defense of the Mission regarding its involvement with the persecutions. In the body of the document, Jones cites chapter and verse in identifying the Mission as the perpetrator of the ten-year-long persecutions. More than that, he scrupulously names numerous individuals who were victims of the kingdom's intolerance. He identifies them by name, age, sex, the charges against them and the various punishments inflicted upon each.

It is clear that the information contained in this document is that drawn upon by Father Yzendoorn in his 1927 *History of the Catholic Mission in the Hawaiian Islands.* If anything, Jones provides additional information, much of it historical. He had been a faithful recorder. He provides such background information as describing the effort of Jean Rives to successfully persuade the Sacred Hearts Fathers in Paris to establish a Pacific beachhead.

In addition to chronicling the events surrounding individual persecutions, Jones devotes ample descriptions to the expulsion of Fathers Bachelot and Short. The exchange of correspondence between ship captains and the government regarding the expulsion is illuminating. Also, official documents on the matter, some signed by Ka'ahumanu, lend substance to the subject.

Correspondence between Kīna'u and the French and Spanish consuls is printed in full in the *Suppliment*. The matter of the Manifesto takes up almost as much space as do the details of the persecutions.

Much of this is firsthand information, and Yzendoorn was fortunate in being able to borrow from one who had been on the scene. Not found in Yzendoorn is Jones' account of the two priests being denied their request for a trial. Also, Jones is informative regarding the details of the arrival at Honolulu of Father Robert Walsh. He states that the Irish Walsh came from "the college of Picpus in Paris on the 30th of September 1836" (*Suppliment*, 20).

Little is known about complaints, if any, by foreigners (read Caucasians) regarding the persecution of native Catholics. But Jones alludes to the displeasure of some foreigners on this matter. At one point in April 1831, "The white residents held a meeting at the Oahu Hotel and, with the two consuls [Jones and British Consul Charlton] as leaders, prepared the following protest to the king… viewing with alarm and the encroachment made on our liberties, religion and amusements we beg to address your majesty and chiefs in council…" (Gast, 138). Nothing came of their complaint if for no other reason than the king, still a minor and one who still enjoyed fun and games, was also virtually without power.

Beyond a doubt the greatest non-Catholic supporter of the Catholic natives, and the priests, was John Coffin Jones. There is no record of any Catholic foreigner taking such a stand. It was Jones who took up the cudgels. In his later years, Jones, his wife Manuela, and their six children retired to his original hometown of Newton, Massachusetts. He continued business ties with California and Boston agents despite failing health. He died in Newton on December 24, 1861, thirty years to the day after writing his letter of recommendation and support on behalf of the departing exiled priests.

He was buried in the Newton Catholic cemetery. "A restless sailor was home from the sea" (Gast, 195).

CHAPTER FOURTEEN

Rites vs. Rights

Months before the 1839 Manifesto forced the government to grant religious freedom, the council of chiefs had been drafting their own document that would come to be known as a Declaration of Rights. They labored long and conscientiously to bring forth statutes that would, among other things, give more protection and privileges to tenants on lands owned by various chiefs.

No longer could a chief say "Begone!" to tenants who had lived and labored on chiefly lands. Much thought was given to other various rights and concerns of commoners and aliʻi alike. Helpful direction was given by the Reverend William Richards who had left the Protestant Mission to become advisor to the young king.

This Declaration of Rights focused not only on land rights but also on such matters as water and irrigation rights, taxes, a civil code and many other mundane matters. But there was no mention of religious freedom in the kingdom. Little did the chiefs, or Richards, know that this issue was only a matter of months away, when Laplace entered Honolulu harbor, Manifesto in hand.

Less than a year later, the kingdom had brought forth its new—and first—constitution. Built upon the Declaration of

Rights and cognizant of the 1839 Manifesto, the constitution, in its preamble, specified, among other things, that there should be complete freedom in the matter of religion.

Understandably there were pockets of Protestants who found it galling to recognize the rights of Catholics to worship as they pleased, with Roman rites, especially after a decade of official prohibition. Yzendoorn refers to the continuance of "petty annoyances" (142–143). There was no overnight transition toward tolerance.

One instance of vindictiveness happened on the O'ahu land holdings of Chief Abner Paki and his chiefess-wife, Konia. As landowners they assumed, incorrectly, they had the right to decide who would work and live on their vast lands. But the June 1839 Declaration of Rights had given more privileges to land tenants. Yzendoorn explains that "...by the 6th section [of the Declaration] permanent possession of their lands were secured to landholders while they [tenants] continued to pay the rent" (142).

In August 1839, a month after the departure of Laplace, Paki and Konia ordered all Catholic tenants to "give up their lands and all the property they possessed" (ibid.). Twenty-two Hawaiian Catholics were evicted. That very same day the displaced residents marched over the Pali cliffs to take their grievance to Father Walsh at the Catholic mission. They arrived at sundown (ibid.).

Soon, Jules Dudoit, the sympathetic French consul, was involved and lost no time in contacting Paki and Konia. They stood their ground. The following day King Kamehameha III heard of the dispute. "He manifested his displeasure and said he had given full liberty to all his chiefs and subjects, to embrace whatever religion they thought proper" (ibid.). The neophytes were allowed to return to their homes with the guarantees they would not be bothered again because of their religion.

Another "petty annoyance" occurred at a place thirteen miles out of the city. There a Catholic convert had his dwelling destroyed by a Protestant native on the assumption that the householder planned to make it a place of Catholic worship. Informed of this violation of religious rights, the king ordered the dwelling to be restored by those who had demolished it.

Within a few years, practitioners of the Mormon (Church of Latter-Day Saints) faith would arrive in the Islands to further complicate Hawai'i's growing religious diversity. The arrival of ten Mormon preachers in December 1850 created no immediate commotion. But by 1852, "Mormonism had encountered mounting opposition from rival religious factions" (Bishop, 122). Despite the 1839 Act of Religious Tolerance, after more than thirty years of having a monopoly on Christian religious services, Protestant missionaries considered all interlopers as intruders.

Henry Bigler, one of the first Mormon leaders, reported that he "and his associates were to find out that further rivalry for native souls which Mormons offered was not welcomed" (Bishop, 127). As Mormons grew to more than three thousand members, the antagonism of Protestant and even Catholic missionaries, among others, asserted itself against the newly arrived sect. The decision was made by the Mormon missionaries to find a temporary gathering place where they could be unmolested. They chose the Island of Lāna'i.

Even on Maui, Mormon evangelism drew ire. Laboring on O'ahu, Bigler was denounced by a "Calvinist minister," believed to be John Emerson, who saw Mormon emissaries as work of the devil and "flew into passion" in the process of condemning this interloping enemy.

Nonetheless, the Mormons increased in number, and this may well have been a factor that discouraged opposing Protestant missionary resistance from developing beyond individual complaints and harassment.

Also toward the middle of the nineteenth century, the Episcopalian religion made an appearance. It was marked with resistance which would, like the Catholic experience, last about a decade. But unlike the Catholic experience of severe physical persecution, this became largely a war of words, words, words.

Physical punishment for religious beliefs of any kind was not only forbidden by the Laplace treaty, it was now unconstitutional. Prior to that agreement, the Protestant ABCFM had influenced the Hawaiian monarchy even to the extent of promoting annexation to the United States. It had been not only a denominational war, but a quest for political power. The annexation proposal was effectively squashed by King Kamehameha IV (Lunalilo).

An earlier trip to England by Kamehameha IV and his consort Queen Emma stirred their admiration for the English monarchy, and the king was also attracted to the established Church of England. He admired it for its liturgical expression of Christianity and its attitude, which he found less rigid than the Hawaiian Protestant Mission.

Earlier, when the king and his young bride were wed at Kawaiaha'o church (often referred to as the Westminster of Honolulu), the service was officiated by a Congregational minister. But at the couple's request it was celebrated according to the Book of Common Prayer of the Church of England.

Unimpressed by the Honolulu Protestant missionary services, in 1859 both the king and his wife requested Queen Victoria to send to Hawai'i clergy from the established Anglican Church. To keep it free from any sign of officialdom, the king offered to provide the land for the church and to pay from his personal funds for a cleric and housing. He also expressed the desire that his young son (also a Kamehameha), be christened with the name of Prince Albert Edward Kauikeaouli Leiopapa, and be instructed in the teachings of the Church of England. (It was their misfortune to have the future king of Hawai'i die at the age of four.)

Robert Wyllie, foreign minister for the kingdom of Hawai'i, let his English counterpart, Manly Hopkins, know that the promotion of the English church in the Sandwich Islands was personally sponsored by the king and had no ties to the Hawaiian government. Such an action would have been unconstitutional. (The Scottish-born Wyllie had earlier arranged to have the children of Anglicans baptized by arranging with the chaplains of visiting British ships to perform the service.)

The agreed plan was to send a clergyman as well as a bishop, whose rank and authority would, it was hoped, lend strength to the founding of the new church in Hawai'i. The plan had the blessing of Queen Victoria.

In time, a capable bishop was assigned to lead the venture. The Reverend Thomas Nettleship Staley was a Cambridge graduate and an educator of distinction in England. He was also a strong advocate for the poor and he possessed an affection for indigenous people.

But before Staley set sail, word was out among the Hawaiian Protestant Mission that there would soon be holy competition from England in Hawai'i. Words began to fly to and fro across the Atlantic Ocean. The person who represented the highest post in the ABCFM was the Boston-based Reverend Rufus Anderson, high potentate and longtime foreign secretary for the ABCFM. Aside from objecting to the presence of another Christian denomination, the ABCFM saw this as a move on the part of the British to establish Hawai'i as a colony for the crown of the expanding British Empire. Down deep within Anderson was the lurking fear that the entry of a competing religion would seriously diminish the political power of the Hawaiian mission, something it had enjoyed since 1820.

Also disturbing was the similarity in rites and rituals between the Episcopal Church and the Roman Catholic liturgy. Shades of resurgence in "Popery" raised the ire and fears of the Protestant leaders. Such a situation nearly demolished diplomatic relations between Great Britain and the Hawaiian kingdom. But by this time, forty years after the expulsion, the

Roman church was established and gaining converts. The days of Calvinist exclusivity were at an end.

Chief among Anderson's objections was that he had been led to believe that only a single cleric would come to establish the Church of England in the Pacific. When he learned that no less than a consecrated bishop was also coming to help establish this foreign church, Anderson raised the religious roof. Blistering letters flew between the New England office of the ABCFM and the Church of England, but to no avail.

Upon Bishop Staley's arrival (with his sole cleric) he had no welcoming party to greet him, not even the nucleus of a congregation. He and his wife had seven children for whom to care and provide schooling. After laboring ten long and difficult years in the field, Bishop Staley returned to England, but not until a successor bishop picked up what was a still-struggling Anglican church. Before Staley departed for England he had the satisfaction of baptizing Queen Emma, who had been instrumental in persuading the English church to seek souls in her Sandwich Islands. Her husband, King Kamehameha IV, deep in his grief over the loss of Prince Edward, occupied himself by translating the *Book of Common Prayer* into Hawaiian.

This new church preferred to call itself "The Hawaiian Reformed Catholic Church." It was a poor choice insofar as public relations went. It was a lightning rod that elicited strong Protestant suspicions that the Pope, with a book of Catholic rites in hand, was just around the corner in the cloak of an English church. (It was said that Bishop Staley's relations with the Catholic church in Hawai'i were congenial.) Staley had had no problems with the government functionaries, leaving the Calvinists to see their formidable political power become seriously diluted.

Surprisingly strong opposition to the Anglican efforts in Hawai'i came from Samuel L. Clemens, better remembered as Mark Twain. He had spent several months in the Islands as a writer for the *Sacramento Bee*. His frequent *Letters from the Sandwich Islands* had harsh words for the Episcopal endeavors. He referred to that denomination as "the Royal Hawaiian Church, otherwise the 'Reformed Catholic Church,' a sort of nondescript wild cat religion imported here from England" (Day, ed., *Letters*, 124.). Clemens' attacks on Bishop Staley were misstatements of facts and faith, this despite the fact that Staley and Twain had never met.

The Reverend Rufus Anderson, from his east coast ivory tower, continued the war of words. Attacks in Honolulu's major daily papers (Protestant owned and oriented) continued. But the Episcopalians had established a small beachhead. It was a determined and faithful group, however small, that enabled this European newcomer religion to survive.

The premature death of King Lunalilo, said to be brought on by grief over the death of his young son and heir, was a serious setback for Hawai'i's fledgling Episcopal Church. Attacks from the Puritan sector did their sanctimonious best to undermine this newcomer. Even though Bishop Staley left Hawai'i after several years of "making a decision for Christ," he left behind a firm rock for his successors to stand upon.

As for the Catholics, even with the Laplace treaty and the Religious Tolerance Act, Catholicism had a hard row to hoe. It struggled for many years not only in Honolulu, but also in rural districts. The influence and domination of so many Protestant ministers in comparison to the sparse number of French priests weighed heavily in favor of the former. It was a situation which would continue for several years.

Chapter Fifteen

The School Problems

To their credit, the Protestant missionaries put the matter of education at the top of their list of priorities. This was in keeping with the instructions given the Pioneer Company that sailed from Boston for the pagan Sandwich Islands in 1819. The American Board of Commissioners for Foreign Missions urged missionaries to cover the islands with farmed fields, schools and churches, and to promote reading and writing, in order to acquaint the native people with the Bible.

True, the original schools were no more than grass huts with wooden benches and the schools were few and far between. As more missionaries arrived more "stations" were established and next came a school. True to their instructions, the missionaries taught the natives to read and write, and soon qualify as teachers—of a sort.

It was early on, in 1825, that the missionaries established a school upland from the seaport village of Lahaina, Maui. It was a boarding school for Hawaiian boys who soon came to know not only their letters and the Bible, but arithmetic. The latter would serve them well in years to come when surveying lands was a necessity as well as an honorable occupation. But in its early days, Lahainaluna school provided enough of an education to young Hawaiian males to enable them to qualify as teachers. The school was founded in 1831 and for many years was a Protestant establishment which turned out some accomplished students. It is considered the first school of any size west of the Rockies. (Today it is a public school, co-educational and is supported by the State Department of Education.)

After the French Treaty of 1839, the Catholic priests were well aware that they could now openly preach the word of God as Catholics saw it. Slowly, the number of Catholic priests increased as ordained members of the Sacred Hearts fathers were sent forth from Paris.

Understandably, they were not welcomed by the Protestant Mission which for twenty years had had the playing field to itself. Well before 1840, the Hawaiian government (with direction from the Protestant missionaries) was in charge of the school system.

The ABCFM was very much involved, as was its right, in drawing up what would be known as the school law of 1840, even to the point of financial support, however meager, for the native teachers. Now, with some degree of regulation and monetary aid, these schools spread slowly through the islands. Known as government schools (instead of public schools), they struggled along with the best teachers they could find and such printed matter as the Mission Press could turn out. One of the books that most schools possessed and taught from was the Bible. The New Testament was expounded by the Protestant ministers and Lahaina seminary graduates. In short, these government schools were basically Protestant when it came down to such fundamentals as faith and morals.

The Catholic priests (there were no Catholic lay teachers for some time) were not long in setting up schools of their own. Friction with the government schools was bound to surface. One bone of contention swirled around the government teachers' certificates, documents that the government issued.

No doubt that some of the Catholic lay teachers did not measure up to standards set by the government. But ecclesiastical cries of prejudice came from the Catholic clergy who saw Protestant hands denying certificates to those candidates bound for Catholic schools. Yzendoorn pointed out that those who were responsible for issuing the certificates were teachers from the Lahaina (Protestant) school (156). That same school, as well as the Mission Press in Honolulu, was also responsible for the various printed tracts which spouted "anti-papist" teachings.

As for the books in the common schools, the Protestant minister Armstrong "made it a point to furnish every child with a copy of the New Testament...Books of the Hawaiian common schools were calculated to insure the pupils with hatred of and contempt for Catholics" (ibid.).

Father Maigret wrote to his superior in Paris that "The Calvinists continue to make every exertion to prevent the progress of the Catholic religion. With this view they have dictated to the Chiefs of these islands laws tending to place all the authority in the hands of the pupils of the Protestant high school...All those who henceforth, will be charged with teaching, must come from this school, or at least be approved of by those who direct it."

Among the bright spots that encouraged the Catholic clergy in its own proselytizing role was that "The King seemed to approve of the course Father Maigret was taking, for he declared his willingness to grant a piece of land, if a Catholic high school should be established. Without waiting for the grant, Father Maigret lost no time in establishing a Normal School on the premises of the mission at Honolulu."

On May 21, 1841, the chiefs, troubled by the constant friction between the two systems, met at Lahaina in an endeavor to resolve some of the differences. One of the more positive results was to eliminate the word "missionary" from those Protestant individuals teaching or otherwise connected with the common school system. In its place these individuals would be known as "school agents."

This change, however commendable, did not over night resolve the ill will of individuals who still resented the presence of Catholics in any part of the overall school system.

One of these new school agents was a young man named David Malo, who much later came to be recognized as an eminent historian and scholar. Malo is described by Yzendoorn as an ardent adherent to the Calvinist tenets. But the Protestant missionary, the Reverend John Emerson, was more pointed. He was, said Emerson, "a man of strong character, deep and earnest in his convictions, capable of precipitate and violent prejudices, including to be austere, and at times passionate in temper" (179).

About 1841, two years after the French treaty allowing freedom of religion for all, Malo was the school agent for the district of Lahaina. Once in Wailuku when "the new Catholics refused to send their children to sectarian public schools, the school agent [Malo] began to enforce the law of May 21, 1841 which, as we have seen condemned the transgressors..." Provoked at what he considered unlawfulness on the part of the neophytes "...he began kicking about a little boy and by tieing [sic] the hands of the child behind him" (ibid.).

Following this, Malo rounded up about one hundred catechumens, including children, had them tied together, two by two, and marched them all the way along the long, hot dirt road to Lahaina. Once there the prisoners were given only salt and nonis, a very insipid fruit usually consumed only in time of famine. They were then conducted by Malo to the district governor, one Auhea. This individual informed the prisoners that they had not been arrested because of their religion "but because they had refused to send their children to the Protestant schools." About this time, the king (Kamehameha III) "who had seen the troop of Catholics passing by, sent three officers to enquire what was going on. Having been informed of the facts he expressed his dissatisfaction, in consequence of which the prisoners were released on the next morning" (ibid.).

Yzendoorn reported that as a result of this event twenty converts were the fruit of the day. Malo would have been sorely distressed at this turn, but one speculates as to why he, as the school agent for Lahaina, took upon himself a matter which belonged in the affairs of the Wailuku school agent.

Malo was an educated and informed individual, yet he was content to ignore that portion of the 1839 Treaty which clearly stated that the members of the Catholic church shared the same rights and privileges as Protestants.

Surprisingly Samuel Kamakau, who would later become a renowned historian, took a path not unlike Malo's. He willingly led a crusade against the few Catholics living in the small village of Kīpahulu in southern Maui. Yzendoorn says that "this co-disciple of David Malo [both had attended Lahainaluna school together] accompanied by a numerous troop of followers, and entering into the houses of the Catholic converts, robbed them of all they had: poi-pounders, hatchets, calabashes, clothing and so on. This species of confiscation he inflicted upon the Catholics in accordance with a custom called 'Hao,' by which, previous to the time that the people had written a code of laws, the high chiefs had the power to strip a wrongdoer of all his property" (Yzendoorn, 181). Kamakau also destroyed a little chapel which a Catholic named Kekuaau had built there.

Some of the dissension abated when the king, in 1843, made a tour of the islands. He found the occasion to improve the picture by stating that, though he was a Protestant and was unhappy to see so many of his subjects embracing another religion, nonetheless he put forth a proclamation declaring it was his will "that all his subjects dwell together in harmony." Unfortunately he went on to say that, "Protestantism is the religion of the State" but did express his hope "that all his subjects would be tolerant of other religions" (168).

Government-appointed district school inspectors were known to have denied teaching certificates to numerous would-be Catholic teachers.

Much dissent occurred in four small towns in North Kohala, on the very tip of Hawai'i Island. The situation in the mid-1800s was chronicled by Patricia Alvarez in *The Battle of Wai'apuka School: One Round of an Epic Contest*. The author writes that "this small village...was the unlikely venue for an important educational struggle of the nineteenth century. That struggle pitted American Congregationalists and politicians against French Catholic missionaries." It was also noted that "The school skirmish [at Wai'apuka] mirrored a larger battle being waged in Honolulu and elsewhere with Catholicism staking out a place for the ideas of church–state equality...the priests [in Hawai'i] were at a great disadvantage..."

A low Catholic presence was reflected by the preponderance of Protestant influence not only in the school districts on all islands but also in the legislature and other government bodies. School laws of 1840 were patterned after the Massachusetts system of the 1600s which ordered that all children from age four to fourteen attend schools which, of course, were Puritan in structure and teachings.

Some of the earlier Protestant missionaries serving as members of government educational boards, such as the Reverend William Richards, were for "giving Catholics a square deal." Years later it came to pass, but not without Catholic persistence—and from high places. One was the French consul Guillaume Dillon who was, apparently, so zealous on behalf of the French priests that the Protestant missionaries were successful in having his government recall him. The practice of generally having Congregational teachers in the public schools was to continue for several years. Catholic schools were initiated in some of the smaller towns, such as Wai'apuka, but attendance was minimal, so much so that some did not survive.

It may have been an uphill fight for the "Papists," as they were still called, but they sometimes did have the support of such eminent non-Catholic leaders as historian Abraham Fornander who sent his daughter to a Catholic school for girls in Honolulu.

Happily for all concerned, there were no serious differences when it came to allocating public funds. The government school system "recognized the right Catholics have to a fair and just proportion of the funds appropriated for the common schools, as long as with it they do the same thing that is done in the common schools" (174).

Yet between the Protestant-focused public schools and the Catholic-oriented schools, it would be a long time before there would appear any neutral schools.

Afterword

Persecution of Catholics in any form ceased officially the day the Laplace terms were ratified. Not only was punishment of native Catholics terminated, but freedom to worship in any religion became law. Wrote Kuykendall, "Persecution had passed forever and none but ordinary difficulties had to be coped with. These difficulties, however, were not inconsiderable" (105).

Understandably there were Protestants who found it difficult to recognize the rights of Catholics to worship and preach as they pleased, especially after a decade of official prohibition. Yzendoorn refers to the continuance of frequent "petty annoyances."

Though petty annoyances did not disappear overnight, they were not reserved for the Catholics alone. Apparently the Catholic missionaries themselves, now protected by the weight of law, at times felt justified in trying to intimidate Protestants.

One instance of alleged, and believable, arrogant behavior is recounted by the Reverend Titus Coan in his book *Life in Hawaii* (Coan, 99). Coan was a highly respected individual and an eminent preacher. Most of his ministry was on the Island of Hawai'i where he was more or less the dean of the Protestant clergy. His residence in Hilo saw many visits from clergy of his faith and those of other faiths. When a French frigate dropped anchor at Hilo, the consul and Catholic bishop on board "made a polite call at our house," he wrote.

Renowned for spreading his faith, he is said to have converted more than seven thousand natives, thus making him one of the most successful preachers in Christendom. The historian A. Grove Day claims that such a large number of converts made "it the largest Protestant congregation in the world" (Day *Biographical*, 24). That many later dropped out is no reflection on Coan's considerable influence in Hilo and the widespread districts of Puna and Ka'ū.

Coan's other interest was in the behavior not of natives, but of the very active volcano of Kīlauea. He led several trips to Kīlauea's edge, many for scientific purposes, as little was known about volcanology at the time. His notes and observations have been of inestimable value to scientists even to this day, since almost all that is known of volcanic action from 1835 to 1865 is found in Coan's articles to the *Missionary Herald* and the *American Journal of Science*.

It was probably on one of his trips back from Kīlauea that Coan encountered firsthand the arrogance of an over-zealous Catholic priest. After citing a number of incidents where Catholic priests had openly told Protestant natives they were definitely on the wrong track and were doomed to perdition unless they accepted the "true church," Coan had his own experience. Returning to Hilo from Wai'ōhinu, "as I was passing a Catholic church under the foot-hills of Mauna Loa I was stopped by about two hundred Catholics, headed by a French priest who challenged me then and there to a debate. This was in a narrow pass along the road which was so completely obstructed by the collected Catholics as to prevent my passing on. The challenge I respectfully declined, as it was late and I had some eight or ten miles of rough road to travel before I slept. I begged the mob to suffer me to pass peacefully [sic]. This the priest refused, commanding the people to keep the passage blocked, and with lifted hand and clenched fists he declared that this man Coan, this opposer of the Catholics, should never pass until he had accepted the challenge of debate."

The challenged preacher declined again and again, asking for passage through the crowd for himself and his small party. Meanwhile, the priest "became furious and his whole frame trembled...while the people around him seemed fierce as wolves." Coan writes that he then descended from his horse and tried to elbow his way through the crowd. "The priest kept right before me with his hands quivering and voice roaring: 'Who is the head of the church?' For a time I made no reply but quietly tried to make my way along, till at last I spoke out in full and clear tones 'Jesus Christ, He is the head of the Church.' Immediately the priest roared out at the top of his voice, 'That is a lie! Peter is the head of the Church.'"

That was enough for a Hawaiian named Samson, one of Coan's small party and someone Coan describes as having the voice of a giant and the arm of Samson of old. Samson cried out, "Clear the road and let my teacher pass!" And with that, his strong arm scattered the crowd "and a passage thus opened" (Coan, 96ff.).

But the holy and effective evangelist that he was, Coan was not to be free from "intruders." Almost immediately after describing his confrontation with the Catholic priest he wrote, "Not many years after the introduction of the papal priests came a drove of Mormon emissaries [1850]. These spread themselves in squads all over the group [of islands] like the frogs of Egypt." Coan, however, never earned nor deserved the reputation of being hostile to the Catholic clergy.

With the establishment of the Catholic, Mormon and Episcopalian churches, the day dawned when Hawai'i was no longer a Calvinist stronghold. But opposition to Catholic progress was found at sea as well as on land. When one of the priests sought passage to New Zealand, the captain, a Protestant American, "refused to carry thither any Catholic priests" (Yzendoorn, 114).

Two years after the Laplace affair, the Protestant missionaries were understandably still rankled at having the treaty rammed down their collective throats. In October 1840, when the U.S. East Indian Squadron anchored in Honolulu, the Protestant missionaries saw this as an opportunity to lay their case before Commodore Read. They got short shrift from the commodore who not only ignored their letter of appeal but sent a reply in which he recommended "the utmost forbearance as the best and only means of disarming your opponents of any resentment they may feel...." In short, the commodore washed his hands of the matter.

At this point the missionaries took their grievance to the head of their home country, the United States Congress. This "Missionary–Memorial" as it was known, was referred to the Department of State which took no immediate action on the matter (139).

With the hope that the French king, Louis Philippe, might set things right, the Memorial was passed on to a Mr. Baird, presumably in the American Diplomatic Service in Paris. In February 1841, Baird was successful in obtaining an audience with the king of France, "to whom he presented a letter of the Prudential Committee on the matter of the Missionaries versus Captain Laplace" (ibid.). The king presented his own case and it was to tell Baird of "his regret that the chief of the Sandwich Islands had not at once permitted the Catholic missionaries to remain there and do what they could, without infringing their laws, to promote their religion." King Louis Philippe could not see, he said, why this could not be allowed. He expressed the opinion that both religious denominations were "infinitely better than none." He expressed the hope that "Catholic and Protestant missions might go on everywhere together in a spirit of harmony and good will."

But, while harmony and good will may have been a goal after the Laplace Treaty, it was not without sad exceptions, particularly on the outer islands where some authorities were not fully informed as to the religious rights of Catholics. Official persecutions may have ended but there were several cases of harassment, some serious. While the police on those islands were not sufficiently informed that Catholics must be left alone, just the opposite occurred on Kaua'i. A policeman was discharged from the force for having attended a Catholic service. At the same time, an unnamed work overseer was dealt the same "punishment," for being present at a Catholic service.

On the small westward island of Ni'ihau, resentment ran high when Father Walsh attempted to plant his religion there. Here, too, official word as to the terms of the Manifesto and subsequent treaty apparently had not been circulated. Though Father Walsh had baptized over one hundred Ni'ihau natives, resentment flourished. A private home which had been converted into a chapel was broken into and its altar demolished. Some nearby lumber for construction of a bona fide chapel was "shivered to pieces" (178). The same treatment was shown several months later when two constables were ordered to destroy an already completed chapel.

On the island of Moloka'i, a Catholic convert, with the very Catholic name of Dionysius, refused to labor on the construction of a Protestant church. Whoever was in charge summoned the police. The authorities, probably not informed of the newly gained rights of Catholics, arrived on the scene. Taking unnecessary and drastic steps they tied the hands and feet of Dionysius together and slung him horizontally from a pole, apparently readying to take him to the local jail. In the process they were none too gentle for, in carrying him suspended from the pole, they broke the back of their victim. Yzendoorn reports that they loosed the ties of the man and took him home "where he vomited blood profusely" (168). Death was not far off and the question has been asked if Dionysius was not a martyr for his faith. (One assumes that a Catholic priest gave the Hawaiian man the name of Dionysius at the time of his baptism. No doubt the newly baptized

Hawaiian took the name of the third century Dionysius who lived in Rome, became a priest and later pope.)

As time progressed there were bright spots on the horizon for Catholics endeavoring to establish their churches and schools, especially where communication had been slow in reaching officials on the neighbor islands. On Kaua'i, the inspector of schools, after examining the students of Father Walsh, "publicly manifested his satisfaction with the progress they had made. He gave the priest an assistant teacher and appointed three school trustees" (177–178). A few days later, after examining the students, the inspector found them proficient "in reading and arithmetic."

Over the years, while harassment surfaced from time to time, considerable Roman Catholic progress was much in evidence. This was especially due to the arrival of the Sacred Hearts Sisters from France in 1859. Their numbers added to the same French order which already had several priests and brothers in Hawai'i.

In 1883, five Franciscan Sisters from Syracuse, New York, established themselves under the leadership of Mother Marianne Cope, who was later known for her aid to the victims of Hansen's disease on O'ahu and Moloka'i.

They were soon followed by the priests and brothers of the Marianist order from Dayton, Ohio, who today are the teachers at Saint Louis High School and Chaminade University in Honolulu.

Each of these religious orders set up schools on the three major islands of O'ahu, Maui and Hawai'i. None were co-educational then and some remain single-sex today. There are presently forty-four Catholic schools in Hawai'i, of which seven are high schools.

According to the 2001 *Official Catholic Directory*, individuals who identify themselves as Catholic represent approximately twenty percent of the state's population of 1.2 million.

Much of the remaining eighty percent of the Hawai'i population belongs to other Christian denominations, including the Church of Latter-day Saints (Mormons). Buddhists and practitioners of several other religions such as Baha'i and Islam make up a substantial part of the total population. Members of the Jewish faith have a temple in Honolulu and are also represented on each of the three major neighbor islands.

The harmony that exists today throughout Hawai'i's many faiths, churches and temples is a tribute to the leaders of those faiths in this multiethnic state. In 1940, when Bishop Stephen Alencastre died, the old rivalries were nowhere to be seen. At the hour of his funeral Mass in Our Lady of Peace Cathedral, the bells of nearby St. Andrew's Episcopal Cathedral tolled in mourning.

Appendix

The following twenty-five names are those listed in Yzendoorn as having suffered persecution by imprisonment and/or hard labor at the hands of the Hawaiian government during the period of 1829 to approximately 1839. Page numbers are referenced in Yzendoorn.

1. Luika Kaunaka   p. 53
2. Pulcheria   p. 53
3. Valeriano Hinapapa   p. 53
4. Akeroniko   p. 54
5. Alokia "and seven others"   p. 57
6. Agatha Kamoohula   p. 79
7. Philip (Pilipo?)   p. 83
8. Helen   p. 83
9. Ailimu   p. 83
10. Kilika   p. 85
11. Lahina   p. 85
12. Marianna   p. 89
13. Malia Makalena Kaha   p. 89
14. Julianna Makuwahine   p. 89
15. Pelipe Mokuhou   p. 68
16. Kikime Kaihekauila   p. 68
17. Pakileo Lukini   p. 68
18. Nanakea   p. 68
19. Kekila Kakou   p. 68
20. Monika Ai   p. 68
21. Kaika Kapuloaokalani   p. 68

It is established that many more Catholics suffered persecution but their names are not known.

It is not unreasonable to believe that during the period of persecution well over one hundred Catholics suffered for their faith. As Yzendoorn writes, "These confessors deserve to have their names recorded as on a roll of honor" (68).

Bibliography

Alexander, William De Witt. *A Brief History of the Hawaiian People.* New York: American Book, 1891.

Alvarez, Patricia. "The Battle of the Waiʻapuka School: One Round of an Epic Contest," *Hawaiian Journal of History* 33 (1999): 1–20.

Annales de l'Association de la Propagation de la Foi: Recueil Périodique des Lettres de Évêques et des Missionaires des Missions des Deux Mondes...Collection faisant suite à Toutes les Éditions des Lettres Édifiantes. 6 vols. Association de la Propagation de la Foi: Paris, Lyon, 1826–33. Vol. 4.

Bancroft, Hubert Howe. *History of California.* Vols. 18–24, *The Works of Hubert Howe Bancroft.* San Francisco: A. L. Bancroft, 1884–1890.

Bingham, Rev. Hiram. *A Residence of Twenty-One Years in the Sandwich Islands, or, The Civil, Religious, and Political History of those Islands: comprising a Particular View of the Missionary Operations connected with the Introduction and Progress of Christianity and Civilization among the Hawaiian People.* Hartford: Hezekiah Huntington, 1847.

Birkett, Mary Ellen. "The French Perspective on the Laplace Affair," *Hawaiian Journal of History* 32 (1998): 67–99.

Bishop, Guy. "Henry William Bigler, Mormon Missionary to the Sandwich Islands During the 1850s," *Hawaiian Journal of History* 20 (1986): 122–7.

Chamberlain to Evans, Honolulu, 22 February 1937. Papers of the American Board of Commissioners for Foreign Missions 31 No. 27, Houghton Library, Harvard University.

Coan, Rev. Titus. *Life in Hawaii: An Autobiographic Sketch of Mission Life and Labors (1835–1881)*. New York: Anson D. F. Rudolph, 1882.

Daws, Gavan. *Shoal of Time*. New York: Macmillan, 1968.

Day, A. Grove. *History Makers of Hawaii, A Biographical Dictionary*. Honolulu: Mutual Publishing, 1984.

————, ed. *Mark Twain's Letters from Hawaii*. London: Chatto & Windus, 1967.

de Freycinet, Captain Louis. *Voyage autour du Monde…1817, 1819 et 1820…*. Vol. 2. Paris: Chez Pillett, Aine, 1829.

Ellis, Rev. William. *Journal of William Ellis: Narrative of a Tour of Hawaii, or Owhyhee: with Remarks on the History, Traditions, Manners, Customs and Language of the Inhabitants of the Sandwich Islands*. Honolulu: *Honolulu Advertiser*, 1963.

Fornander, Abraham. *An Account of the Polynesian Race. Its Origins and Migrations*. Vol. 2. London: Trubner, 1880.

Gast, Ross. *Contentious Consul*. Dawson's Book Shop: Los Angeles, 1976.

Hawaiian Mission Children's Society (HMCS). *Missionary Album: Portraits and Biographical Sketches of the American Protestant Missionaries to the Hawaiian Islands*. Honolulu: Hawaiian Mission Children's Society, 1969.

Hawaiian Mission Press (HMP). *He Hoikehonua* [A Geography]: *he mea ia a hoakaka'i i ke ano o ka honua nei, a me na mea maluna iho*. Honolulu: Na na Misionari i Pai [Hawaiian Mission Press], 1832.

Hinds, Richard Brinsley. "The Sandwich Islands, from Richard Brinsley Hinds' Journal of the Voyage of the Sulphur (1836–1842)," ed. E. Alison Kay, *Hawaiian Journal of History* 2 (1968): 102.

Kamakau, Samuel M. *Ruling Chiefs of Hawaii*. Honolulu: Kamehameha Schools Press, 1961.

Kane, Herb Kawainui. *Voyages*. Honolulu: Whalesong, 1991.

Korn, Alfons, transl. "Shadows of Destiny: A French Navigator's View of the Hawaiian Kingdom and its Government in 1828," *Hawaii Journal of History* 17 (1983): 1.

Kuykendall, R.S. *The Hawaiian Kingdom*. Vol. 1. Honolulu: University of Hawaii Press, 1938.

Laplace, Cyrille Pierre Théodore. *Campagne de Circumnavigation de la Frégate l'Artémise, Pendant les Années 1837, 38, 39 et 40, sous le commandement de M. Laplace*. 6 vols. Paris: A. Bertrand, 1841–1854. Vol. 5.

Reynolds, J. N. *Voyage of the United States Frigate Potomac: Under the Command of Commodore John Downes, during the Circumnavigation of the Globe, in the years 1831, 1832, 1833, and 1834; including a Particular Account of the Engagement at Quallah-Battoo, on the coast of Sumatra; with all the Official Documents Relating to the Same*. New York: Harper & Brothers, 1835.

Schoofs, Rev. Robert. *Pioneers of the Faith*. Honolulu: Sturgis Printing, 1978.

Semes, Robert Louis. "Hawaii's Holy War: English Bishop Staley, American Congregationalists, and the Hawaiian Monarchs, 1860–1870," *Hawaiian Journal of History* 34 (2000): 113–38.

Silverman, Jane. *Kaahumanu—Molder of Change*. Honolulu: Friends of the Judiciary History Center of Hawaii, 1987.

Suppliment [sic] *to the Sandwich Island Mirror, containing an Account of the Persecution of Catholics at the Sandwich Islands. Remarks on 'An account of the transactions connected with the visit of the l'Artemise; Remarks on the manifesto; and the treatment of the missionaries.' Hawaiian Spectator,* vol. 11, no. 4, article 4. Honolulu: R.J. Howard, 15 January 1840.

Yzendoorn, Father Reginald. *History of the Catholic Mission in the Hawaiian Islands.* Honolulu: Honolulu Star-Bulletin, 1927.

Further Sources, as cited by Yzendoorn

Archives of the Catholic Mission, Honolulu.

Bachelot, Alexis. Journal. c. 1826–1837. Vatican Archives.

Bingham, Hiram. *Report to the A.B.C.F.M.,* 1830.

Bondu, Melchior. Journal c. 1827–1832. Vatican Archives.

Dana, Richard Henry, Jr. Letter to the *New York Tribune,* 5 June 1860.

The Friend (Honolulu). February 1860.

Kamakau, S. M. 'Moolelo o Kamehameha I,' *Ka Nupepa Kuokoa,* No. 265, 29 December 1866.

Maigret, Louis. Journal, c. 1832. Vatican Archives.

The Polynesian (Honolulu). 28 October 1841.

Sandwich Island Gazette (Honolulu). 7 July 1839, 22 June 1839, 25 June 1839.

Wyllie, Robert C. "Historical Summary," in *Report of the Minister of Foreign Relations* [to the Nobles and Representatives of the Hawaiian Kingdom]...*1853.* Honolulu: Department of Foreign Affairs, 1853.

Index